THE HUMAN ELEMENT
IN LITERATURE

The Human Element in Literature

By DANIEL EDWARD PHILLIPS

(Professor of Mathematics and Associate in Psychology, Shepherd
State Teachers College, Shepherdstown, W. Va. Formerly
Head of Department of Psychology and Education,
University of Denver)

FORTUNY'S

NEW YORK

THE HUMAN ELEMENT IN LITERATURE
Copyright 1940 by Daniel Edward Phillips

FIRST EDITION

Manufactured and Printed in the United States of America

CONTENTS

PREFACE

LITERATURE is life. Psychology claims to reveal life. Can these two statements be true and yet travel two different roads? If they are true they should have much in common. It is this common background of human nature and literature that has interested me for many years, and on which I have tried to collect material for a quarter of a century. In 1913, I first printed in *An Elementary Psychology* a chapter on "Psychology in Literature."

On reading Goethe's *Sorrows of Werther* I was struck by the similarity of the background ideas there and in James' *Psychology*. The more I have read and studied the more I have become convinced that any piece of literature is great and lasting in proportion to how well it handles the psychological principles of human life.

On the other hand it has long been evident that some rejuvenation of the teaching of literature is badly needed. An examination of books on literature reveals an overwhelming emphasis on technique. Next to this stands the appalling fact that knowledge *about* literature is often exalted above *inner appreciation of literature*. Efforts to standardize and formalize have destroyed the soul of literature. The only substantial value of literature is inner appreciation—the feeling that it expands your own life.

It is these two strong convictions that have led me to offer to the public the outstanding conclusions of these many years of study. This work makes no effort to be exhaustive and even hundreds, or perhaps thousands of pieces of literature not mentioned, may be cited as a good or better representation of the idea.

This is a pioneer work and we feel sure that much

greater things will follow along this line. Modern literature has become consciously psychological. Yet students
fail to become acquainted with the modern biological
idea of original nature.

There is a voluminous literature that aims to explain
the works of a writer by his constitutional nature and
by the psychological happenings in his life. These works
shed much light upon the works of literary geniuses,
but we shall be concerned only incidentally with that phase
of the problem.

Again, the manner and extent to which any given
genius reflects the ideas and feelings of his time has not
yet been given the definite psychological explanation that
it deserves.

But our field of inquiry is largely untouched. *We are
to inquire into how far some of the outstanding works
of literature contain and develop the principles and laws
established after many years of scientific psychology.* In
other words, have literary geniuses become what they did
because they naturally had a deep insight into human
nature? If psychology is only a scientific study of human
nature, and if literature of a universal type represents the
deep and permanent phases of human life, the two should
meet somewhere. Our hope is to develop a new attitude
and a new method in the study of literature. We hope to
produce a book that may be serviceable to students of
both literature and psychology as well as to the general
reading public.

At the close will be found my grateful acknowledgment
to authors and publishers whose books have been helpful
to me in this work. I must also acknowledge my indebtedness to Kitty Hodges for assistance in the preparation of
the manuscript and correction of proof.

Shepherdstown, W. Va.   D. E. Phillips.
Feb. 1, 1940.

THE HUMAN ELEMENT
IN LITERATURE

CHAPTER I

HUMAN NATURE IN MUSIC AND ART

LET US SAY once and for all that we are converts to the doctrine of evolution—that everything in the universe is evolving from simpler forms. This applies to music and art, two of the most ancient forms of the intellectual and emotional life of the race. Music and art have left their marks upon all peoples at all times. Their roots strike deep into the human soul. They are so universal and so ancient that no great thinkers have been able to agree concerning either their history or their mental origin. All archaeological discoveries have revealed evidence of these human developments.

MUSIC—THE HEART OF HUMANITY: Music is the deepest and most universal language of the human heart. There is no emotion that cannot be expressed by music and its twin sister, the dance.

Music may have preceded spoken language. Intelligible language greatly aided the evolution of music; yet music developed a language all of its own in the meaning of its variable rhythms.

The association of ideas and feelings we put into *Old Black Joe* and *Swanee River* profoundly modifies and deepens the effect of the songs on us. And their rhythm grips and holds millions who do not know the language. In the same way the *Beer Barrel Polka* has its own language, and the moaning of the wind in the forest and the strange music of frogs in the spring of the year speak individual languages.

He who would understand the human heart must know universal music and the growth of folklore into songs, dances, myths and primitive poetry, together with something of their hidden meanings. In music, tones are substitutes for words. Melodies make sentences, and themes grow into large conceptions of life and philosophy. Design is full of meaning and even folksongs have their crude designs.

The sensuous side of music is usually first conceived, but great composers have expressed the deepest psychological thinking by music, and a few, like Wagner, have used both poetry and music. Here in music, just as in art, the three psychological functions of sensuous, intellectual, and associative impressions may combine to produce the most intense form of musical appreciation. Wit and humor are about the only psychological qualities that music does not give us. For more definite and elaborate treatment see Howes' recent book on *The Borderland of Music and Psychology*.

There is a marked gap between the musical notes of animals and the music of man. Man alone has resorted to objective means of expressing his inner life through music. Man alone has been able to vary rhythms voluntarily to suit his inner life.

After centuries and centuries passed, the growing complexity of man's life progressed from mere sound to speech of some kind. The expression of his internal life by the dance, poetic expression and the construction of crude musical instruments. Subsequently others began to recognize these feelings because they had within themselves the same *possibilities*. This is true today when we read what we call a great piece of literature. It is to us really great only in so far as it seems to be an expansion of ourselves.

PSYCHOLOGICAL BACKGROUND:—This background remains in obscurity. Three leading theories have been offered. The first theory was that of Darwin.[1] Then Spencer held that *song* and *dance* were, in their origins, an exaggeration of the innate language of the emotions— that all music is an idealization of human passions. In 1893 Richard Wallaschek's *Primitive Music* was published. He held that music evolved out of the rhythmical impulses in man.

In 1896 John Dewey claimed that the number concept is only that of *ratio*.[2] My own researches on the origin of the number concept, published the same year, lead me to the conclusion of a serial origin not only from bodily rhythms but also from the rhythm of day and night, from moon periodicity, from man's own footsteps, etc.[3] Yet that in itself is not music.

Here we encounter the same difficulty as we do in dealing with human *drives* or instincts of hunger, sex, self-preservation, fear, pugnacity and imitation. They are so complex and interrelated that their simple origin is hidden from us.

Throughout the history of music a few things stand out which express the deepest thoughts and feelings of humanity. This expression has been largely personal and unconscious. Again, the dance and poetry early became a part of music. Some kinds of illustration, drawing and painting soon became sisters of music. However, we must not leave this universal creative impulse of the race without tying it to one of the greatest tendencies of present day education. Rousseau's cry of back-to-nature was misinterpreted and poorly applied until the recent development called Creative Education.

Without arguing about origins, let us accept the universal evidence that one of the deepest and most far-reaching urges of humanity has been the impulse or tendency to *create for the sole pleasure of creating*. This creative act results in intensified emotion which gives joy in accomplishment. It is not equally strong in all peoples. As Rugg puts it in *The Child-Centered School,* the creative impulse is well-nigh universal in children. It is the same thing which both Rousseau and Tolstoy saw in human nature.

Creative Education is on the right track. I hold that the average child of today has as strong an urge to create as did primitive man, if only we give him opportunity and stimulus. To quote from Kilpatrick:[4] "All in some manner create, the few in high degree. Creation is peculiarly the work of the self and person as such. There can be no truer respect for personality than to expect and encourage creation. And creation enriches life. Nor is creation confined to 'art.' All life demands it and illustrates it."

This stands out as our natural introduction to any serious consideration of world literature. Any psychological account of man that neglects these universal and natural developments must remain inadequate no matter how scientific the experiments may be. The psychology of humanity transcends the laboratory.

FOLK-MUSIC:—We have a chance to study primitive music in existing savage tribes and in folk-music. Only a few years ago interest in folk-songs and dances spread through the civilized nations and took its place in our educational system. In them we begin to trace the evolution of rhythm, melody, harmony, and color tone, the leading elements of all music. All these have been the subject of experimental studies in our laboratories.

Indian tribes have songs for love, war, work, hunting, spring, summer, harvest, canoes, clothes, lakes, rivers, etc. The Indian always sings the song suitable to his occupation and to his station in life.

We know more about the Indians through our rich

collection of Indian songs and dances than we know in any other way. Their songs and dances constitute the chief part of their lives. Song is their poetry as is primitive poetry elsewhere. Mothers teach their children geography and the life of their peoples through song. The Medicine Man likewise teaches through song. He who would know humanity in primitive life must know that the song is primitive literature. Stevenson's *Home Book of Verse for Young Folks*[5] illustrates the psychological relation between song and poetry in modern life. Here you will see the past and present meet. Only make a list of the great world literatures, of symphonies and musical dramas, of the great themes of artists—founded on primitive folk-lore—and you will begin to realize that a deep meaning lies behind these semi-conscious manifestations.

THE DANCE AND RELIGION:—Kirstein's recent and comprehensive book on *The Dance*[6] gives the following remarkable statement from the Chinese as to the origin of dancing: "Under the stress of joy, man makes words. These words are not enough; he prolongs them. The prolonged words are not enough; he then modulates them. The modulated words are not enough, and without even perceiving it, his hands make gestures and his feet begin to move." He finds that in every part of the world, regardless of climate or other outside influence, there is a striking similarity in all early human activities. The normal human being expresses his emotions by means of the song and the dance, all after a similar pattern. These roughly divide themselves into the social aims and the religious.

MUSIC AND THE ANCIENT NATIONS:—We know that four thousand years ago on the banks of the Nile in Egypt music was an art. It seems likely that Pythagoras, the founder of Greek music as art, carried some of the elements of Egyptian music to Greece. These two nations developed music to a high degree of perfection. With the Greeks, music became identical with literature and to some degree with philosophy. Even mathematics was reduced to a question of harmony. However no great number of musical instruments has been found, although in Egypt numerous drawings and paintings of musical instruments and musicians have been discovered.

China early developed a science of music. As early as 2277 B.C. there were many writers about dances and music. Confucius in 551 B.C. speculated concerning the origin and function of music.

But of most interest to our purpose is the likeness of ancient Chinese music to Peruvian music and to that of the Aztecs of Mexico. The possibility of a borrowed element cannot be denied. But it is the elements of humanity which they have in common that we are looking for. Is it not plausible that human beings are constituted so that under similar conditions they produce similar results? Primitive music and dance have everywhere been methods of expressing deep, personal emotions. In so far as they are dominated by similar emotions, the manifestations will be similar. They pave the way for poetry and world literature.

HINDU MUSIC: The material on Hindu Music is very extensive, but like all other Hindu developments, we first encounter it in a relatively high state of maturity. The invention and beginning of music are attributed to the gods. Man received his instruction from the heavenly dancers. Even in ancient Vedic times many musical instruments were in use.

The Rāmāyana and Mahābhārata began to take form about 1000 B. C. They contain many references to musical performances. In the former we find the following:

"Actors gay and nimble dancers, singers skilled in lightsome song, with their antics and their music pleased the gay and gathered throng."

In the Mahābhārata we read:

"Dancers charm the gathered people,
Singers sing and actors play,
Fifteen days of festive splendor
Greet the concourse rich and gay."

GREAT MUSICIANS — A PSYCHOLOGICAL ENIGMA:—Genius is a stumbling block for the psychologist, especially for those who deny the influence of heredity and rely upon physiology. The difficulty is outstanding when we attempt to explain the precocious musical genius. If Rousseau presents such a mystery that his biographer says he was one personality when he tramped about southern France and sent his children to a foundling institution and a different one when "he arose to a kind of a divine ecstasy" during the writing of the *Social Contract* and *Emile*—what, then, shall we say of Mozart who, when only six years old, not only knew music, but composed it and made a tour of Europe where his performances became the sensation of the hour?

Or how shall we explain that giant intellect of Wagner whose genius took in not only the largest conception of music, but also included social problems, literature, and philosophy? Here was a man who wrote his own poetry for his world dramas. Here is a man who conceived the great psychological drama of human life from its beginning to its grand philosophic future.

His songs and dramas are the work of a literary genuis of wide grasp. *The Nibelungen Ring* is not one but the ingenius combination of various myths and ancient traditions; he wove them into one great harmonious whole. The ancient spirit or psychological development we have been following is preserved, but it all develops into the mantle of modernism. Finally social philosophy takes the place of ancient mythology.

> Sudden the sky was lighted with red glow,
> Like many great auroras swift it spread:
> The towers of fair Valhalla were aflame,
> Circled with fire the gods and heroes sat;
> And men beheld it in a speechless awe.
> Fiercer and higher leaped the heavenly fires,
> Valhalla was enwrapped in sheeted flame;
> Valhalla, built by might and bought by guile,
> Its sovereign god forsworn and desolate,
> His hopes laid low, his fondest purpose foiled;
> Valhalla, grounded in the greed of gold
> And garrisoned by fear and base deceit.
> At last, the dreadful day of doom had dawned,
> The curse had worked its wrath, despair and death;
> At last, the twilight of the gods had come,
> And Wotan's loveless kingdom was at end;
> At last, the gathering night had covered all,
> The cruel reign of loveless law was done,
> Now dawned the day of nobler men and deeds,——
> For the new world of love's great law began!

Lest I should seem to be extravagant I quote the following from Huckel:

"There is something primitive, colossal, majestic in Wagner's fourfold music drama of *The Nibelungen Ring.* It partakes of the power and grandeur of the earlier ages of the world. It is a drama of the mighty era of the gods, the giants, and the heroes before the coming of man upon the earth. It is the wondrous story in which was enwrapped much of the religious belief of our ancient Northern ancestors in Europe.

"The deepest truths of this drama of primitive life are universal, and their meanings as potent today as in the prehistoric world. It is a vast allegory of the strongest passions of life. It is a dream of yesterday and a vision of tomorrow if we have the eyes to look into the heart of its mystery."

We might well apply what we have been saying about the difficulty of understanding musical genius to Beethoven, Schubert, Listz, Chopin and scores of others; but our object throughout this work is to use only a few of the best illustrations to show human nature in world literature. Wagner was one, if not the first, to apply a universal psychological principle to the comprehension of the human struggle.

MUSIC APPRECIATION:—All great achievements in music have a story, a theme lying behind them. The story may not be told in words. Neverthless it is there. It is a psychological blunder for an instrumental musician to give a performance without an explanation of the emotions and thoughts lying behind the composition. It is a mistake to assume that they will be grasped by the listener. Music appreciation is like appreciation of literature. *It is individual.* No one can make you *feel* that certain music is great just by saying so, but suggestion about the thoughts and feelings hidden in it may lead to a wider appreciation

The radio has made music a psychological possession for all peoples in all lands.[7] The imagination cannot picture the profound change that radio has produced on peoples all over the world. In the last fifteen years, it has stimulated and modified the feelings and thoughts in all lands. Wherever music is broadcast, there is need for some explanation of the meaning of all serious productions.

CHURCH MUSIC:—Church music as here used is different from the universal religious song and dance. Church music came down to us from the Jewish synagogue. It was much modified by the Greeks. It later reached a high development in the monasteries of the East. One of the most interesting things about church music is the psychological manner in which the words are made to express the faith and beliefs of a given order. A student of human nature could doubtless collect a large number of church song books and determine the various denominations simply by their content.

Religious songs of peoples reveal their views of life. Thousands of lines like these could be collected: "This world is a wilderness of woe. This world is not my home." Some social psychologist has gone so far as to say that the melancholy lying behind all Hawaiian music is the echo of a dying race. It is James Cabell who suggests that every heaven that has ever been created in the world came out of what he calls the demi-urge to *romance*.

My psychological criticism of our church music is that it smells too much of the graveyard. Most of it was written in times of tragic doubt and social suffering, greater than we know now. I often wonder if it is necessary for religion to be melancholy. Or, if we lose the serious or melancholy aspect, will we lose religion?

This psychological study of music and dance has been presented as a preparation and background for the larger and more definite aspects of world literature. But it will not be complete unless we present some ideas of *art* in the form of painting.

PAINTING AND ITS PSYCHOLOGICAL SIGNIFICANCE:—Painting is an original urge of humanity. Although Leonardo da Vinci held that the art of painting is the widest of all the arts, it has by no means been as universal as have music and the dance. When and where painting began no one knows.

Specimens of painting are found in ancient China and India. Their oldest literature contain many evidences of the art. Many very ancient buildings of Egypt, Greece, and India show that the art flourished in the dim dawn of the race. Even the caveman of Europe and the yet unknown ancestors of the American Indian understood the art of symbolizing things and events by painting.

Evidently painting required a fairly high degree of skill, patience, and symbolic thought. These made it a far more specialized art than music and the dance. Yet the whole American continent from Alaska to the South shows evidence of this art. The totem poles of Alaska, with their strange significant figures and paintings speak a language not yet understood. Not only are these poles which are erected in front of houses decorated from bottom to top, but the roofs and walls of houses are also decorated. These totems preserve family and tribal history.[8]

In southern Colorado there are evidences of the Cliff Dwellers in the painted rocks. Even before the government took over the Cliff Dwellings, I entered underground chambers by way of a shrewdly concealed passage. Here was a dome shaped room, large enough to hold forty or fifty people, and painted and decorated in the brightest colors. It may have been a church or a council-chamber.

In Central America all pottery is highly colored and decorated. The decorative patterns are evidently significant and indicate a culture of a complex nature. The Mayas and Aztecs took delight in symbolizing the human figure.

However, we must not close this chapter without glancing at the big language, history; and themes, yes, philosophy, lying behind the great conceptions of masterpieces of art.

There was a time when not even the language of religious stories was known to the masses. They may have heard these stories read from the Bible, but they knew them better from the great paintings of Raphael, Leonardo da Vinci, Angelo and other masters. In many cases Turner [11] shows how paintings are made to teach real history. They then become a form of literature. The *Battle of St. Egidio* by Paolo Uccello will far outlive the historic descriptions.

PSYCHOLOGY IN PAINTING:—The last topic for our consideration is the manner in which painters transfer their psychology to paintings and make us feel it. They express every human emotion: joy, longing, and heart ache. When will our psychologists, who experiment and talk much about how patterns of various kinds are built up out of environment, *explain how great paintings become the universal patterns for all people in all time*. These patterns, like those common to music and the dance, while not exactly the same, have a common impulse or urge behind them.

THE SPELL OF MUSIC AND ART:—For many years one of the chief psychological problems has been the mental effect of music and painting. It is the old Greek problem of *beauty* and its effect, to which Ruskin paid much attention. When we ask what this beauty is good for we may as well ask what *life is good for*. There is no answer but *the urge to live* itself.

Is the one who appreciates music, painting, and literature any better than the man of low taste? Such a question can be answered only by the man who has experienced both. But thousands of experiments show that there is the possibility in man of a higher and wider appreciation.

This psychological *spell* seems to unlock the possibilities of the creative genius of the race. Investigations have been made concerning the *spell* under which geniuses do their work. Many say they must get in the work-spell by listening to stirring music, by communing with the silence, by the moanings of the sea or forest.

So we stake this as our first discovery of human nature in world literature: The main thing that lifts human nature above all other creation is this spell of appreciation, of even primitive creative ability and its stimulating effect both on the producer and appreciator as an *end in itself*. Outside of food and sex it is the one thing that expresses the real urge to life, the heart of humanity.

Having presented this general chapter on literary stories, music and art, as a general background revealing the deep underlying trend of human nature, we will proceed to show the more specific and daily elements of human nature in world literature and to compare these findings with modern psychology.

CHAPTER II

HUMAN NATURE IN WORLD STORIES

MUSIC IS PERHAPS the most universal form of expression for the emotions, desires and urges of the human heart. Next to music stands religion. The third great psychological universality is stories. All the world loves a good story. The psychology of short stories is usually so simple and their play upon the feelings and imagination so capable of variation as to be adaptable to all time and all ages. Neither story telling nor story writing is learned from grammar and rhetoric. It is the naturalness and spontaneous obedience to the psychological laws of association and play of emotions that make the so-called laws of the story. They are in reality laws of the mind.

The most lasting and powerful stories of the race have come out of the ages, from the early spontaneous development of the ancient civilizations. India, Persia, Arabia, Palestine, and Greece will always be famous for their stories. It is doubtful if any story of its kind ever has or will surpass the story of Joseph and his Brethren. Like most early stories it was probably current long before it was committed to writing. Its play on instinctive jealousy, on parental affection, on the universal mystery of dreams, on curiosity, and on imagination all combine to produce a psychological fascination. It is found in the thirty-seventh chapter of Genesis. Like some Hindu stories it begins with the jealousy of half-brothers. Jacob had twelve sons. Ten of them were half brothers to Joseph, whom the father loved more than all his other children. The ten brothers hated Joseph, plotted his murder, but finally sold him as a slave, and made the father believe that he had been devoured by wild beasts. The Mideanites sold him in Egypt, where he was later falsely accused and cast into prison. Through his interpretation of Pharaoh's dreams he became ruler of the land.

On one hand the story plays on jealousy and on the other kindness, tenderness, and sympathy. It shows that underneath the evil impulses lies the better side of human nature. No one is wholly good or wholly bad. Nothing could be more natural or more touching than the scene where Joseph reveals himself to his brothers. One must naturally wonder what rules could have guided these early and powerful creations of the human mind. Evidently it was that same creative urge for the expression of inner life which we found in the previous chapter.

"Then Joseph could not refrain himself before all them that stood by him; and he cried, 'Cause every man to go out from me.' And there stood no man with him, while Joseph made himself known unto his brethren. And he wept aloud: and the Egyptians and the house of Pharaoh heard. And Joseph said unto his brethren, 'I am Joseph; doth my father yet live?' And his brethren could not answer him; for they were troubled at his presence.

"And Joseph said unto his brethren, 'Come near to me, I pray you.' And they came near. And he said, 'I am Joseph your brother, whom ye sold into Egypt. Now therefore be not grieved, nor angry with yourselves, that ye sold me hither: for God did send me before you to preserve life. For these two years hath the famine been in the land: and yet there are five years, in the which there shall be neither earing nor harvest. And God sent me before you to preserve you a posterity in the earth, and to save your lives by a great deliverance. So now it was not you that sent me hither, but God: and he hath made me a father to Pharaoh, and lord of all his house, and a ruler throughout all the land of Egypt. Haste ye, and go up to my father, and say unto him, Thus saith thy son Joseph, God hath made me lord of all Egypt: come down unto me, tarry not: and thou shalt dwell in the land of Goshen, and thou shalt be near unto me, thou, and thy children, and thy children's children, and thy flocks, and thy herds, and all that thou hast: and there will I nourish thee.' "

Stories are variously classified. For our psychological purpose we offer four groups, each to some extent overlapping the others:

1   Simple narration of actual or imaginary occurences.
2. The story intended to produce a definite psychological and ethical effect.
3. The story dominated by some specific and definite psychological or philosophical principles.
4. The highly figurative, subtle story, permitting and suggesting a wide range of psychological ideas and often pervaded by keen sarcasm.

1. The simple narrative story exhibits some simple psychological machinery. It utilizes long standing customs, traditions, and beliefs. In modern psychological language it has a good apperceptive background.

In the second place the simple narration permits free mental activity. From childhood to old age free mental play with feelings and ideas is always a source of pleasure. Directed school work and examinations destroy most of the free mental play of the mind.

Again, such free narration stimulates and gives new life to the instinct of *curiosity*. It becomes an outlet for a blocked instinct. Curiosity is the bud of intellect, and imagination of emotion. Again let us insist that neither simple story telling nor big story telling in literature has been guided by any conscious rules. They came out of the natural constitution of the human mind. Our rules are simply looking backwards. Doubtless the story teller originally got more joy out of watching the effect produced on the listeners than they did.

We will now examine a few types of such stories as we have in mind under this first division. It is unfortunate that we must either make only brief quotations from most works or resort to some kind of condensation.

Homer's *Odyssey*[10] will go down through the ages as representing all we have said about this first class of stories. It contains complete stories within a story. One is where Ulysses, in his wandering, is shipwrecked on the Phaeacian Island. Here we have the free play of imagination and emotion. Here we see human nature and human instincts laid bare. Curiosity soars on wings of its own.

Now turn to *Don Quixote* and examine it for all the points we have mentioned. Read the story of *The Diamond Necklace,* by Maupassant. An undertone of emotion and curiosity carries you with increasing intensity to the end. There with a bang that echoes in you for days you are dropped.

The power of the simple narrative story is often the psychological charm of autobiography. Goethe's *Truth and Fiction Concerning My Life* holds a double charm of half-concealed and half-revealed truth. It is one of the most fascinating artistic conceptions ever penned. To the many questions as to whether this or that happened he replied that it is not a question of what did happen, but of what might have happened. Cellini, the Florentine sculptor, gave to the world one of the most charming autobiographies ever written. Rousseau's autobiography has been pronounced a psychological enigma when taken in connection with his literary achievement, but Cellini's is none the less so and gives a more vivid impression of reality. This strange genius has been described as egotistical, industrious, courageous, a pleasant companion, self-reliant, but also as cruel, vicious, religious, a cutthroat, and a villain. All these he relates with simplicity and a sense of realism not felt in many autobiographies. Its psychological effect is one of wonder and amazement.

If any one still doubts the natural urge to sympathy let him read Maxim Gorky's *My Childhood*. It is all touching and emotional but most of all where he relates Grandmother's instructions to God concerning the whole family.

"Grandmother gave to God a circumstantial account of all that had happened in the house. Bowed down, looking like a great mound, she knelt, at first whispering rapidly and indistinctly, then hoarsely muttering:

" 'O Lord, Thou knowest that all of us wish to do better. Michael, the elder, ought to have been set up in town—it will do him harm to be on the river; and the other is a new neighborhood and not overdone. I don't know what will come of it all! There's Father now. Jaakov is his favorite. Can it be right to love one child more than the others? He is an obstinate old man; do Thou, O Lord, teach him!'

"Gazing at the dark-featured icon, with her large, brilliant eyes, she thus counselled God:

" 'Send him a good dream, O Lord, to make him understand how he ought to treat his children!'

"After prostrating herself and striking her broad forehead on the floor, she again straightened herself, and said coaxingly:

" 'And send Varvara some happiness! How has she displeased Thee? Is she more sinful than the others? Why should a healthy young woman be so afflicted? And remember Gregory, O Lord! His eyes are getting worse and worse. If he goes blind he will be sent adrift. That will be terrible! He has used up all his strength for grandfather, but do you think it likely that grandfather will help him? O Lord! Lord!'

"She remained silent for a long time, with her head bowed meekly. and her hands hanging by her sides, as still as if she had fallen asleep, or had been suddenly frozen.

" 'What else is there?' she asked herself aloud, wrinkling her brows.

" 'O Lord, save all the faithful! Pardon me—accursed fool that I am—Thou knowest that I do not sin out of malice but out of stupidity.' And drawing a deep breath she would say lovingly and contentedly: 'Son of God, Thou knowest all! Father, Thou seest all things.' "

The author says: "I was very fond of grandmother's God Who seemed so near to her, and I often said:

" 'Tell me something about God.' "

The universal psychological effect of such a story has no explanation except in the deep storehouse of original nature.

2. The second group of stories are those intended to produce a definite psychological and ethical effect. Literature is full of them, especially religious literature. No writer has made so consistent a use of the story for this purpose as Tolstoy. While he discarded all the miraculous in religion, he took the Sermon on the Mount and all its teachings literally and believed that a moral law should have no exception. To this end he wrote many *Gospel Stories* with an unusual simplicity and force.

What Men Live By[11] is a wonderful story of brotherly love.

When Tolstoy wrote *Resurrection* specifically in support of the Sermon on the Mount, he received many severe criticisms, especially concerning "forgive your enemies." His reply was the powerful story—*The Long Exile*.[12]

This is the story of one Aksenof who stopped at a way-side inn, and paid the innkeeper the night before as he must leave early. About noon as he rested under some oak trees officers arrested him for killing the man in the adjoining room. They found the bloody butcher knife in his bag. Although his wife begged him to confess and escape going to Siberia, he firmly said: "In the name of God I cannot confess myself guilty of a crime I did not commit." He was sentenced to a life time of servitude in Siberia. After twenty-six long years have gone by and all have come to love "Grandfather," a newcomer, Makar, is ushered into camp. As each one save Aksenof tells the offense for which he was sent to prison, it becomes evident to "Grandfather" that the New Comer is the one who killed the man and put the knife in his bag.

Aksenof is sorely tempted to kill the New Comer. He cannot sleep, but the next morning decides not to tell nor to kill him. Two weeks later Aksenof passed by the new comer's bunk and saw him creep out from under the bunk, where he had been digging under the wall. He cautioned the old man not to tell and he would take him out also. Or if he did tell, he would kill him.

The next day the officers discovered the new dirt and asked each man if he knew who was digging the hole. All denied any knowledge of it. Then the chief officer said to Aksenof: "Old man, you are truthful. We have all learned to love you. Tell me before God who did this." The old man hesitated a long time. Then the officer demanded once more: "Old man, tell me the truth. Who dug that hole?" Then the old man said: "I cannot tell, your Honor. I will not tell. Do with me as you please; I am in your power."

Makar confessed his crime.

When they came to let Aksenof go home, he was dead.

Perhaps many will praise the old man for his supremely noble deed. At the same time they may confess themselves unable to do likewise. Our contention is that such literature is psychological and touches the deep universal urges of humanity.

3. The third class of stories is closely akin to this group, but is still more consciously psychological. For example, not many years ago Olive Schreiner wrote definitely psychological stories. These stories[13] specifically aimed to set forth dominant urges, instincts, and the psychological changes due to maturity and sexual conditions.

The Lost Joy is a brief description of how sexual love becomes sympathy. And the wise old woman answered: "O fools and blind! What you once had is that which you have now! When Love and Life first met, a radiant thing is born, without a shade. When the roads begin to roughen, when the shades begin to darken, when the days are hard, and the nights cool and long—then it begins to change. Love and Life will not see it, will not know it—till one day they start up suddenly, crying, 'O God! O God! we have lost it! Where is it?' They do not understand that they could not carry the laughing thing unchanged into the desert, and the frost, and the snow. They do not know that what walks beside them still is the Joy grown older. The grave, sweet, tender thing—warm in the coldest snows, brave in the dreariest deserts, its name is Sympathy; it is the Perfect Love."

Her *Three Dreams in a Desert* represents woman's struggle for freedom and self expression. *The Hunter* brings us face to face with the dominant biological urge for knowledge and self expression. It is similar to those powerful lines in *Faust:*

"O blest, whom still the hope inspires
To lift himself from error'd turbid flood!
What man knows not, is just what he requires,
And what he knows he cannot use for good. . . .
Slow sinks the sun, the day is now no more;
Yonder he hastens to diffuse new life.
Oh, for a pinion from the earth to soar,
And after, ever after him to strive."

Here is a condensed form of *The Hunter:*

In a certain valley was a hunter who went forth to
hunt wild fowl. One day it chanced that as he stood on
the shore of a great lake, a shadow fell on him, and he
saw a reflection in the water. He looked up to the sky;
but the thing was gone. A burning desire came over him
to see that reflection once more. He waited and waited until
night, but it did not return. He went home moody and
silent. To his near friend he said: "I have seen today that
which I have never seen before—a vast white bird with
silver wings sailing in the everlasting blue. It was but a
reflection in the water, but now I desire nothing more on
earth than to hold it." His comrades said he was mad
and would make himself a wonder by claiming to see what
others could not. All said: "Come, let us forswear his
company."

He walked alone and sought in the forests, but he
could not find her. But he shot no more wild fowl: what
were they to him now. One night as the hunter sat weeping an old man stood by him and he said: "Who are you?"
"I am Wisdom," said the old man, "but some men call
me Knowledge. No man sees me until he has sorrowed
much." Then the hunter cried: "Can you tell me what is
that great wild bird I have seen sailing in the everlasting
blue? They would have me believe she is a dream, the
shadow of my own head." The old man smiled: "Her

name is Truth. He who has once seen her never rests again. 'Til death he desires her." And the hunter cried: "Oh, tell me where I may find her." But the old man said: "You have not yet suffered enough," and went away.

After some days, the hunter cried out in bitterness: "And I must sit still and be devoured by this great burning?" The old man, seeing that he had suffered and wept much told him that he must leave the valley of the past forever, that he must wander down into the Land of Absolute Negation and Denial, that mountains of stern reality would rise before him, that beyond them lies Truth. Then the hunter cried: "I will hold her fast, hold her in my hand." Wisdom shook his head. "You will never see her, never hold her. The time is not yet." Wisdom then told him that, wandering in the high regions, he might chance to pick up now and then a white, silver feather dropped from the wing of Truth. The hunter said: "I will go." But Wisdom detained him: "Mark you well—who leaves these valleys never returns. Though he should weep tears of blood seven days and nights upon the confines, he can never put his foot across them. Upon the road there is no reward offered. The work is his reward."

The hunter crept away into the woods. It was growing dark about him; he wandered into the land where it was always night; it was also night in his heart. Finally a faint light played against the horizon, and ere long he stepped into the broad sunshine. In the distance the towering mountains rose up before him. At the foot many paths ran up; he chose the straightest one and began to climb; the rocks and ridges resounded with his song. "It is not so steep as they said," thought he. "A few days, a few weeks, a few months at most, and then the top." But soon the path grew steeper, he needed his breath for climbing and the singing died away. Now also the path began to grow dim, and he made one for himself, until he reached a solid wall of rock. He began to build a ladder out of stones, but not many of them would fit. All the while he kept saying to himself: "Once this wall is climbed, I shall be almost there."

At last he came to the top. Far below him rolled the white mist over the valleys he had left, but above him still towered the everlasting mountains, immeasurably high now. High above him played the eternal sunshine. He bowed himself to the earth, uttered a wild cry, and walked on. No sound was heard save the sound of his tool which rang night and day upon the iron rocks. Years passed over him, still he worked on, and the wall towered above him toward heaven.

As twilight settled down, the Echoes of Despair peeped out from holes in the rocks and cried: "Stop your work, you lonely man, and speak to us. See what lies there, white bones! A brave and strong man climbed to these rocks. He looked up and saw there was no use. So he lay down there and went to sleep forever." The hunter laughed fiercely and the Echoes of Despair slunk away, for they cannot stand the laugh of a brave, strong heart.

After awhile the hunter's shrunken face looked up at the eternal mountains rising to the white clouds. His work was done; he folded his tired hands, and lay down by the precipice where he had worked away his life. Below him over the valley rolled the thick white mist. Once it broke and with his dying eyes he looked down upon the trees and fields of his childhood. He heard people singing as they danced. Once great tears gathered in the hunter's eyes, and he cried: "They who die there do not die alone." Then the mist rolled together again, and he turned his eyes toward the mountains. "I have sought," he said, "but I have not found her. Where I lie down worn out, other men will stand young and fresh.

By my steps they will climb; they will never know the name of the man who made them. At my work they will laugh. But they will mount, and on my work. They will find her through me. 'No man liveth unto himself and no man dieth unto himself.' Then slowly from the white sky came something falling, falling, falling. Softly it fluttered down and dropped on the heart of the dying man. It was a feather.

What are words and definitions of truth, duty, obligation, and character, as compared to such deep-going impulses as this story gives birth to in one's soul! Here it is that we realize that:

> "Sound understanding, judgment true,
> Find utterance without art or rule."

Here we feel the power of Nietzsche's saying: "But the worst enemy thou canst meet will always be thyself. Thou shouldst be ready to burn thyself in thine own flames: how canst thou become new, if thou hast not first become ashes!"

In some professions many are early married to rules and detail. Work and life become a matter of bare routine. They think only of reaching some harbor by a steady application of the oars. I do not belittle such activities, I know they are important. Growth has always been from without inward. In religion all people move from forms and ceremonies to inner states of the individual. In education we pass from the ornamental to the useful, from the externally useful to the internally appreciative and truly inspiring.

Complete stability checks evolution in the line in which it occurs. So progress, growth, development, evolution, always mean change—continual change. Likewise failure or inability to change and adapt to new conditions ultimately means death. Here we encounter the supreme dilemma. The law of progress requires not only occasional but constant adjustment to ever-changing conditions.

Voltaire attacked the problems of his day from a strictly psychological standpoint. For this he spent years in prison and was exiled from his country. One of his most definite psychological weapons is the story, *Zaire*. It is an illustration of the power of environment to make our political and religious beliefs. It is in every sense modern psychology. A very small child is stolen by the Mohammedans and taken to Constantinople. There she grows to maturity—a beautiful and attractive woman who becomes one of the influential wives of the Ruler. During the war on Constantinople many prisoners are captured. Two of them turn out to be Zaire's own father and brother. Finally it happens that, if Zaire will renounce her religion and position she may save her father and brother. Or, if they will swear allegiance to the Mohammedan religion and government, they may live. But so powerful has become their psychological *set* that neither will do so.

This was an anticipation of much of the social psychology today. Hundreds of other stories could be presented. But our object is not a complete survey—*only to establish certain fundamental ideas and types*.

4. Our fourth division of psychological stories is the *highly figurative subtle story, permitting and suggesting a wide range of psychological ideas, and often permeated by keen sarcasm*.

Few writers have equalled Nietzsche in his keen sarcastic use of figurative language. His many brief dissertations in *Thus Spake Zarathustra*[14] constantly puzzle and attract the reader. In that particular it is similar to Omar's *Rubaiyat*. The condensation of thought in both is unsurpassed.

On priests we read: "And Zarathustra spoke unto his disciples and said: 'Seest thou those men coming yonder: Alas, they are mine enemies; but pass them by with sleeping sword. Blood of my blood, they be. They have suffered so much they wish to make others suffer. O, that some one would save them from their Savior.'"

On reading he says: "Another generation of readers and spirit itself will stink."

On one occasion Zarathustra is coming down from the mountain. He meets an old man. He asked the old man: "Whither goest thou?" "I go to the mountains to serve God. Whither goest thou, Zarathustra?" "I go to the valley to serve men." "Men are too vile a thing for me to serve. See that thou givest them only alms." And Zarathustra answered: "Thinkest thou that I am so poor as to give alms?"

Later we shall have occasion to examine in greater detail Browning's *Pippa Passes*. But let us note here its complex underlying psychology. Early in the morning of New Year's Day poor Pippa is looking forward to her only holiday of the year. This poor factory girl spends her day going about singing the songs that lie deepest in her soul. Early in the morning Sebald and Ottima, who have just murdered Ottima's husband, are suffering from a revulsion of feeling. Ottima has just succeeded in diverting Sebald's mind when Pippa passes singing "God's in his heaven." This operates on Sebald's stricken conscience and he kills himself; Ottima offers a prayer for him and does likewise. Later Pippa passes Jules, who, by a trick of his fellow students, has had a woman of inferior rank and blemished reputation thrust upon him as a wife. He is going to desert her. Pippa passes, singing. Jules suddenly decides to let revenge go, to love his wife and seek a new life in her country. In the evening, Luigi's mother is trying to persuade her son not to assassinate the king. She has about succeeded when Pippa passes and sings a song which unconsciously fortifies his wavering purpose. The deed is done. Again, her song prevents Monsignor from carrying out his intention to murder the Intendent of the cathedral palace. The day is spent; she returns to her room at night, wondering if she could ever touch these people "magnificent in sin." She is unconscious of the danger she has escaped from those lying in wait for her, or of the influence she has exerted. And those whose destinies have been sealed by her songs are unaware of the real cause.

Is there any psychology which furnishes us with a better example than this of the power of unconscious suggestion, which gives better proof that life and conduct are under the control of a great network of forces both conscious and unconscious? Psychology is a study of human life; *literature is life objectified and set to the music of other souls.*

CHAPTER III

THE NEW ATTITUDE

THE DAWN OF A NEW DAY:—The dawn of a new day in literature is here. For a quarter of a century a few have tried to encourage a freer study of literature, music, and art and to shake off the chains of formalism. Recently many critics have been pleading that the same freedom and personal appeal that have opened up a new world for them, should prevail in all presentations of literature.

Most of the tendencies to a psychological interpretation of literature appear in indirect suggestions. *What Literature Can Do for Me,* by Smith, develops several such topics in an incidental way. H. G. Wells offers many suggestions on this subject in his recent writings.

Dr. Collins, a physician, has given us a systematic treatment of the subject in his two books—*The Doctor Looks Into Literature,* and *Taking the Literary Pulse.* These books deal with psychology in recent literature, but chiefly with the morbid or abnormal phase. *Modern Fiction,* by Brewster and Burrell, is saturated with psychology. It is a master work. However, there is as yet no systematic effort to compare the findings of great literature with those of modern psychology.

Since the dawn of civilization literature has centered about the great problem of human conduct and never with such tenacity as at present. The Bible is genetic truth because its writers were able to discover the universal in man.

Literature is the life blood of the race: when we are allowed to read literature at the proper stage of development and with absolute freedom of interpretation, it seems actually to be an extension of ourselves. Without being able to name them we realize in ourselves the psychological laws that have swayed the human race. In Goethe's *Sorrows of Werther* we find a clear-cut statement of a fundamental law of all psychology: namely, that mental activity of all kinds is controlled by laws.

FACT FINDING AND THOUGHT GENERATION:—You may find scores of teachers presenting *Silas Marner* in essentially the same way. Let us say that forty boys and girls are studying under one of the best English teachers. A list of questions has been mimeographed and placed in the hands of the students. Not one of the questions refer to the individual ideas and feelings aroused in the students by the reading. They refer to technique, to historic references, to allied works, to a comparison of modern and classical forms of expression, to the conformity to the well-known laws of literature. No sign of intellectual life exists in the response of the pupils. One after another takes up the specific question demanded and either recites some bookish comments or openly and indifferently confesses no knowledge of the topic. One girl ventures to ask an original question. She says: "It seems to me something is wrong with this story." "What is it?" "Why, we hear nothing about Eppie from the time she is nine years old until about sixteen. It seems to me there is time for many things to happen in there." That is the only sign of any personal response.

Let us contrast this procedure with another method. A class had just completed the study of *The Merchant of*

Venice. I was given the privilege of asking the students some questions. I asked the students with what characters they found themselves in sympathy. To my amazement many, if not the majority, replied, "With Shylock." Such a thing seemed impossible and I called on the various groups to defend their sympathy for any given character. The Shylock group replied that Shylock was the under dog, that everyone imposed upon him and took advantage of him, that other people stood up for their religion, and he had a right to stand up for his. I was still more amazed when the teacher offered no interference with this freedom of expression. I remembered my college professor of literature, and how he told us *what* to think about the characters and *why*. He had us search for what others had thought.

Whatever you do, remember that it is not your own personality but the child's that you are trying to unlock. The book should seem an extension of the reader. The chief business of the teacher is no longer to tell the pupils what the literature means to her. We are no longer seeking the injection or inoculation of foreign ideas into the student's mind. We seek an outlet of the indivdual's own soul—*a crystallizing and developing of his own ideas and feelings.*

Many books discuss versification, figures of speech, and classifications of poetry at great length. Professor Miller in his book, *Directing Study,* gives a typical recitation in which the class is called upon to define the various kinds of poetic feet.

I have examined a number of short story books and the model stories which these books present are seldom the stories that grip and hold the reader. They are selected mainly on the basis of technique and formal construction.

Introduce the student to that thundering play *Brand.*

Every page is boiling over with psychological suggestions that inevitably enter the mind of any student trained to think rather than to follow memorized rules.

Literature is filled with the rich content of human nature. Students who are led to make this discovery in literature, have a new and abiding interest in efforts to sound the depths of human nature. This new insight is secured only by permitting free reaction of the individual. Under this freer method, the individual must be led by suggestion and not by dogmatic statements.

THE DEAD EXPLAIN NOT:—The fruitless search for what the author meant should be abandoned. Living writers scorn the idea of explaining what they have written and the dead will not return to do so. And the war as to what the writer really meant goes on. Each is sure he has explained the writer's meaning. One teacher is sure that Shakespeare meant to make Hamlet insane. Another is equally sure he did not. If such students discover anything, it is usually *what some one else said that it meant*.

The more wonderful a piece of literature is the less likely will we be to give any one specific meaning to it. We must give up this fruitless search for definite meanings in great pieces of literature. Each takes on new meaning in different ages and with different peoples. Many have the idea that there is knowledge about literature which is valuable simply as knowledge. The only substantial value in knowing any literature is in its effect on the inner life of the individual.

THE NEW METHOD:—In contrast with these older methods and aims is that new and refreshing point of view taken by Professor Smith in his book *"What Literature Can Do for Me."* Here we have the heart of a new movement in literature. We see that literature must be an outlet for the soul of the individual reader; that it must stimulate and develop the ideal nature of man; that it can and should be one of the chief sources of a definite knowledge of human nature; that it can restore the past as even history cannot; that it can dignify and glorify the commonplace things of life; and that it can give us a mastery of language such as nothing else can furnish.

Every great piece of literature must be true in the sense that given certain conditions the outcome is inevitable— that is psychology.

LAWS OF GRAMMAR, LITERATURE, AND ART:—The laws of grammar, of literature, and art have a *psychological and only a psychological foundation.* They are not laws in the same sense as laws of physics, chemistry, and astronomy. The laws of literature and art are simply mental ways of conceiving things; they are subjective and changeable. So long as human intelligence and emotion vary amongst individuals, races, and different periods of the world's progress, so long shall we be obliged to content ourselves with approximation to any fixed, universal principles. The laws of the physical sciences are objective and are not dependent upon our ways of conceiving them. Two atoms of hydrogen will always combine with one of oxygen to make water, but the formal relations of language have not the same stability.

Ibsen expressed this truth when his great work *Brand* fell a prey to the critics who said he knew nothing about poetry, he replied: "Do not think that I am an arrogant fool. My book is poetry. If it is not, it will be. The conception of poetry in Norway shall be made to conform to the book. *In the world of ideals there is no stability.*" His prediction was more than fulfilled.

CHAPTER IV

HUMAN NATURE AND RELIGIOUS LITERATURE

THE PSYCHOLOGICAL LONGINGS OF HUMANITY:—Should any one read, purely as literature, the ten or twelve great religions of the world, he cannot help feeling that they are all founded upon the same psychological background. Here are some of the universal tendencies found in them.

1. The deep longing for something better—escape from reality—the "demi-urge to romance."
2. A sympathetic consciousness and psychological need of its development for the race.
3. A consciousness of human limitations—the biological mysteries of *life* and *death*.
4. The instinct of submissiveness and desire for leadership.
5. Appeal to the instinct of *curiosity*.
6. The psychological play on the complex and conflicting desires and emotions—especially *love, war,* and *religion*.

Volumes would be needed to develop this psychological background. Here we have space for only a few suggestions.

The two supreme mysteries of humanity have been birth and death. More myths have been created to explain these than anything else. Nearly all religious literature may be classified as idealistic poems born of the quest for something better.

All religions contain ideas similar to the command to Abram: "Now the Lord said unto Abram, Get thee out of thy country, and from thy kindred, and from thy father's house, unto a land that I will show thee." Later we read: "A land flowing with milk and honey."

The shadow of death that hangs over humanity is expressed by Job: "Man born of woman is of few days, and full of trouble. He cometh forth as a flower, and is cut down: he fleeth also as a shadow, and continueth not. And doth thou open thine eyes upon such an one, bringeth me into judgment with thee? Who can bring a clean thing out of an unclean?"

This psychological gloom of humanity has been countered in thousands of ways. Even Job revives from his pessimism with hope for the future. The teachings of Jesus were positive. "In my Father's house there are many mansions: if it were not so I would have told you, for I go to prepare a place for you." In the closing chapter of the Bible we read: "And he showed me a pure river of water, clear as a crystal, proceeding out of the throne of God and of the Lamb—And there shall be no more night; and they need no light neither light of the sun."

The universal similarity of religious thought is one of the most far-reaching discoveries of modern times. It shatters the idea that religious ideas had to be borrowed from some central source of divinely revealed truths. *Everywhere it has become evident that the human mind is so constituted as to develop similar ideas under similar conditions.* Borrowing has taken place, but it is impossible to explain the universal similarity of music, art, religous and philosophic ideas on any ground save that of similar longings, capacities, instincts, and ambitions.

The Hindus grasped our modern idea of a biological urge and expressed it by saying:

"Something compels me, somewhere;
Yet I see no meaning in life's long mystery."

In India the most extensive and original religious poetry developed. All this poetry and all the far-reaching systems of philosophy endeavor to transcend human limitation and stretch out to some unrealized hopes—they would transcend reality.

Buddha plumbed the depths of human nature and even sighted the high points of our modern psychology. In the preface to a work published in 1924, entitled *Buddhist Psychology,* we find these words: "But turn where we will to our manuals of special studies we find no reference to the patient work of many centuries accomplished by the introspective genius of the East. . . . Some of their main contributions are very near the later views advanced by the dominant schools of modern research." [15] Some years ago G. Stanley Hall gave lectures on the psychological ideas of Buddha, and at the close of his *Confessions of a Psychologist,* written just before his death, he named Buddha, Socrates, and Jesus as those whom he revered and worshipped for having best realized the needs of poor, struggling humanity.

Scholars tell us that Buddhist literature covers the best thought and culture of India for centuries, and that it must not be thought of simply as a religion. In *The Gospel of Buddha,* by Carus,[16] we are told that Buddha classified fifty-four tendencies of human beings. This was at least an effort to do what psychology is attempting today—*to label original nature.*

Contrary to the opinion of many poorly informed, Buddha was extremely practical in his teachings. He proclaimed that there is no happiness except in righteousness, that we should not ask about a person's descent but only about his conduct, that health is the greatest of gifts and contentment the best of riches, that we should neither hear nor repeat gossip.

Throughout all religion we observe the desire for something better. Mohammed painted for his soldiers the most sensuous heaven to be found in all literature. The Mormons have the advantage of believing in a progressive revelation pointing the way to the promised land. To them *all religions* are revelations from God, given according to the times, development and needs of the people.

A sympathetic atmosphere and the psychological need for its development is evident in varying degrees in all religious literature. The Sermon on the Mount, the thirteenth chapter of Corinthians, and the whole tone of the teachings of Christ emphasize the development of brotherly love as the supreme end of religion. Although the aim is outstanding in Christianity, other religions are by no means wanting in this tendency.

The great Chinese teacher Lao-Tse taught that God made all things, that spiritual knowledge is innate, that people were once innocent, that they were honest and warm-hearted without being conscious of it, that we should repay injuries with kindness, that there is no absolute and universal distinction between good and bad, that beauty was born with the heavens and the earth, that striving for possessions drives a man to actions injurious to himself and others.

This insight into human nature is not responsible for the degraded religion now known as Taoism in China, any more than the Dark Ages should be considered the outcome of the teachings of Jesus.

The Egyptian *Book of the Dead* is in no wise wanting in its efforts to oppose selfishness, as the following lists illustrate.

General Character—

1. I have not done any injury to mankind.
2. I have not made wretched any cattle.
3. I have not done sin in a place of righteousness.
4. I have not known evil or done wickedly.
5. I have not done each day services ahead of my duty.

Honorable dealing—

1. My name has not come to the boat of the chief.
2. I have not cursed God.
3. I have not caused misery or poverty.
4. I have not done what is abominable to God.
5. I have not made deaf a servant toward his chief.

Avoidance of violence—

1. I have not caused illness.
2. I have not made to weep.
3. I have not killed.
4. I have not given order to cause killing.
5. I have not made deprivation to mankind.

The life, death, and teachings of Socrates will move the hearts of men for all time to come. This could not be true of any one who does not reach the depths of human nature.[17]

And now we conclude this endless effort to combat the selfish instincts of man with the masterpiece of all literature on the subject. The thirteenth chapter of Corinthians may be idealism gone mad, but it will never be surpassed. Its psychology is too deep, too universal, and too lasting ever to be lost by the human race.

"Though I speak with the tongues of men and of angels, and have not charity, I am become as sounding brass, or a tinkling cymbal.

"And though I have the gift of prophecy, and understand all mysteries and all knowledge; and though I have all faith, so that I could remove mountains, and have not charity, I am nothing.

"And though I bestow all my goods to feed the poor, and though I give my body to be burned, and have not charity, it profiteth me nothing.

"Charity suffereth long, and is kind; charity envieth not; charity vaunteth not itself, is not puffed up.

"Doth not behave itself unseemly, seeketh not her own, is not easily provoked, thinketh no evil;

"Rejoiceth not in iniquity but rejoiceth in the truth;

"Beareth all things, believeth all things, hopeth all things, endureth all things.

"Charity never faileth: but whether there be prophecies, they shall fail; whether there be tongues, they shall cease; whether there be knowledge, it shall vanish away.

"For we know in part, and we prophesy in part:

"But when that which is perfect is come, then that which is in part shall be done away.

"When I was a child, I spake as a child, I understood as a child, I thought as a child: but when I became a man, I put away childish things.

"For now we see through a glass, darkly; but then face to face: now I know in part; but then shall I know even as also I am known.

"And now abideth faith, hope, charity, these three; but the greatest of these is charity."

Religion has everywhere been grounded on the two instincts of submissiveness and desire for leadership. Only a universal feeling of helplessness and a longing for some one to lead could account for the hypnotic blindness with which people everywhere have believed and followed the wildest theories and teachings of the race. Under the spell of dominating leaders credulity has no limit. The

world's strictly religious literature belongs to comparatively few individuals whom nature made leaders and
who seized upon the needs of the hour. In a sense all
religions and their development can be explained by the
psychology of suggestion.

Curiosity is embryonic intellect:—Modern education
and psychology are giving it a large field of consideration.
As the reasoning powers of man developed, curiosity
furthered religious inquiry and religious literature attempted to answer the great personal and even biological
problems of humanity. As already mentioned, the universal mysteries of life and death were forced upon
every one. Modern science, instead of smiling at the
crude efforts of man to solve their problems, should pity
humanity, struggling towards the light and then slipping
back into the depths of superstition.

Religious literature everywhere touches complex longings, desires, and emotions. Looked at as a whole the three
great tragedies of the race have been love, war, and religion. Almost an endless number and combination of
feelings are back of each one of these human tragedies.
Nearly all the early literary efforts played upon all three
of these. The Old Testament is a balancing of these three
psychological forces. The great epics of India are built
upon them. Homer's *Iliad* is true to the model.

SUBMISSIVE INSTINCT AND SUGGESTION
IN RELIGION. It is doubtful if any religion could
exist without the universal tendency to submissiveness.
Religions are established by leaders who either possess
superiority or assume it. The endless mysteries that have
confronted the human race plus the helplessness in disease, calamity, and death create in man a feeling of
absolute dependence. Now this universal assumption of
supernatural authority by religious leaders prepares the
masses for *submissive obedience.*

We are not questioning the right or wrong of this submission. We are only stating a psychological tendency of humanity. It may have been necessary to avoid chaos and anarchy. In no other line of human conduct has this submissive tendency been so voluntary, universal, and pronounced as in religion. But even now the growing tendency to dictatorship in government could not exist without this natural submissiveness. The people either do not want to solve their own problems or lack faith in their ability to do so.

SUGGESTION AND RELIGION:—It would not be difficult to write a history showing that religion has been propagated and maintained by the psychological power of suggestion.

Happiness is the chief aim of all mortals, but few if any know how to reach it. He who boldly suggests the way is sure to get a hearing. The suggestion of ease and comfort when you have nothing is appealing. Sickness, disease, and death sadden mankind, yet only the slightest suggestion causes hope to "spring eternal in the human breast."

During the Middle Ages suggestions concerning the Black Death made an insane asylum of nearly all Europe. But we must also remember the irrational conduct of many of our best citizens during the Flu Epidemic in 1918. The most irrational suggestions were acted upon.

Danger and helplessness will cause acceptance of the most irrational suggestions. *So this inherent tendency to submissiveness plus the power of suggestion makes any religion possible.*

CHAPTER V

SPECIFIC AND ALL-PERVADING HUMAN NATURE

VARIABILITY OF MEANING:—Meaning may be direct or indirect, doubtful or without question, concrete or general, practical or suggestive, felt or understood, specific or all-pervading. These possible meanings are always acting and interacting upon each other. The deepest meanings are least capable of definite expression. For example, music touches the deepest things in the development of the human race, yet the only way one can well express what it really means to him is by more music.

WORDS HAVE NO FIXED MEANINGS:—The gradual realization that words have no fixed meanings has done more to undermine religious dogma based on logical jugglery than has any other one thing. The psychology of meaning is fatal to the assumption that there are any fixed laws of literature and art.

The meaning of all words come out of human experience. These meanings did not drop down from heaven. They were not invented by inspired men.

Words are only signs of some mental state which is supposed to be similar in the minds of the various people using them. But they do not give birth to the mental states. I hear my readers say: "What nonsense. For what purpose are dictionaries? Do they not tell us the meaning of words?" No one ever did or ever will get the meaning of a word out of a dictionary. To learn that X means Y gets you nowhere. But if you learn that X is a symbol for human suffering, you know X just in so far as you have experienced human suffering.

During the Middle Ages, formal logic reigned supreme in human speculations, and the whole fabric which it created rested on the assumption of definite meanings for abstract words. Logic is only a delusion when the syllogism deals with subjective, qualitative concepts. This has been the chief blunder of theology for two thousand years.

It is shocking to think that for a thousand years the learned world should have believed that the meanings of words must be secured by the study of dead languages. No dead language or any foreign language possesses any hidden meanings that may be secured by learning these symbols. I once put this question to an advocate of the dead languages: "If I can find twenty-five words the meaning of which you do not know, will you be willing to look up the root meanings and, relying entirely upon those, write an article for a standard magazine using these words?" He saw the dilemma and said, "No." Even if we could arrive at the thoughts and feelings of the Hebrews or Greeks without corrupting them with ours, on what ground can we assume that they had the truth? Such an assumption carries with it the idea of human degeneration. It is a sorry trade that tends to drag us backward instead of forward.

"Thou shalt not lie" would seem to be a law about which there could be no difficulty in giving a universal application. Suppose we should ask, as Socrates did, "Is a lie ever justifiable?" To answer "yes" undermines the law at once. To say "no" involves serious difficulties. Such an answer would be incompatible with any justification of war, for the art of war is one string of deceptions after another. A lie is a qualitative phase of human conduct with no objective standard, and only human feelings and human experiences can put a meaning into the word.

When Socrates received from Thrasymachus the positive answer that a lie is never justifiable, he presented cases such as these: "At the battle of Thermopylae did not our officers lie to the soldiers and tell them that the Spartans would be there in three days? They held the pass and we were saved from slavery. Was that all right?" Again, he asked Thrasymachus if a poor widow has saved her money and buried it in the right hand corner of the cellar, and robbers should come and say: "Madam, have you any money in the house?" should she say, "Yes, in the right hand corner of the cellar?"

The laws of literature and art are simply ways of conceiving things: they are subjective and changeable. So long as human intelligence and emotion vary in different individuals, in races, and at different periods of the world's progress, so long shall we be obliged to content ourselves with *approximation to any fixed universal principles.*

Suppose it be a question as to whether Shakespeare's *Hamlet* or Mark Twain's *Mysterious Stranger* is better. Suppose ten thousand people read the two and only one hundred vote in favor of *Hamlet*. Suppose these are teachers and students of literature. Shall we not accept their judgment as final? But for whom have they spoken? Only for themselves. How can they speak for the ninety-nine hundred unless they can bring them to see in *Hamlet* what they think they see in it? But even then must they not know what the *Mysterious Stranger* has meant to these ninety-nine hundred? Remember that the "best" in any of these fields has no objective standard. That piece of music, literature, or art which does not seem to be an extension of yourself is not suited to you. *It is not best for you and no one can make it best for you by saying that it is best for him.*

The fact that certain pieces of literature have survived is often claimed to be sufficient grounds for pronouncing them the *best*. But have we not evidence in other fields that teaching can perpetuate almost anything?

READING INTO LITERATURE WHAT IS NOT THERE:—Why have we assumed that our chief business is to find out what the author meant by his work rather than what it means to 'us? I can say that Shakespeare meant so and so, but I mean simply that he makes me *feel* that he meant this or that.

The greatness of literature and art consists in the fact that they permit us to read our own spirit into them. The question is not what someone has said that this or that means, but what depths it reaches in us: *what do we feel that it must mean?* It is the standardizing of meanings that has taken us away from the psychology in literature. It has given us the outer knowledge, the form, but it has blinded us to inner appreciation, to the possibility of deep feelings and ideas aroused in us.

PSYCHOLOGY AND THE NEW HUMANISM:— The above position has been attacked by such literary critics as E. P. Moore, Babbitt, and Collins as universal naturalism against which they oppose what they call the *New Humanism*. New Humanism dreads the future and worships the past; behind this movement one recognizes the echoes of deductive thinking for the past two thousand years; in this movement rationalization plays the chief part. It throws psychology overboard as a pseudo-science, yet grounds itself upon psychological assumptions. It does not realize the instability of all subjective standards in literature, art, morals, and religion. It is looking for objective stability where only relative, partial subjective stability exists. The New Humanists would carry us back a thousand years to the theory of innate ideas.

THE PSYCHOLOGICAL ATMOSPHERE:—The sentiments are the chief storehouse of social forces and the chief basis of values. Not long ago I observed a beautiful little church in proximity to a dilapidated old church. The contrast was unpleasant; yet the people who had attended church there so long, sacrificed much to buy the adjoining site and preserve with care this unsightly dilapidated building. This is a *sentiment,* or a group of feelings and their associated ideas, centered about an object.

For thousands of years we have been creating sentiments about individuals, art, literature, and religion, and these sentiments so completely dominate our judgments that absolute truth becomes a psychological impossibility. As a general rule, the probability of getting the truth decreases as age and sentiment increase. Time is one of the chief elements in developing this psychological atmosphere. A multiplicity of opinions, comments, and writings exercise an enormous influence.

Time and the multiplicity of opinions never bring us any nearer to the original meaning, but rather make it all the more obscure. But an interesting phenomenon is that the more this psychological atmosphere, which does not inhere in the work, but in us, increases, the more certain we feel our own interpretation of a great character or work of art to be.

The Bible is a powerful book, but a certain atmosphere is usually identified with its contents. Many are absolutely unable to countenance a critical examination of the book and can never study it as they do other literature. But is there anything in it that prevents such consideration?

Homer's *Iliad* affords another example of this atmosphere. Doubtless it is inherently a great work; but suppose it had been found among the Aztecs or South Sea Islanders, and had thus been stripped of all connection with a powerful and interesting people, and of its three thousand years of study, praise, and adoration? How differently would it appear!

These facts by no means depreciate the inherent worth of these great productions of the race, but only account for our psychological attitude toward them. It shall be our task to point out their psychological fitness to human nature.

BY WHAT STANDARD SHALL WE JUDGE LITERATURE AND ART?—There are only two standards: *what people tell you about it, and what you feel about it*. Unless you tie yourself to what people say, there is absolutely no law save the way in which they appeal to human hearts.

But someone says, "If the cultured and learned decide that any one type is of the highest order, should not this be taught to everybody?" Yes, provided they can be brought to an inner realization of the fact. But here is the stumbling block of our modern conceptions. If this "highest" must be learned as a rule, a dogma, or a mere jumble of words, positively no! It will then only be the means of blinding the individual to all internal appreciation and of leading to a loss of faith in his own inner life.

Literature is great in proportion as it touches the ancient background of feelings, instincts, impulses, longings, and urges of the race. But freedom is necessary in literature in order to produce this powerful all-pervading effect. Indeed this same freedom of appeal to the deep feelings, instincts, and longings is necessary to both the production and the enjoyment of literature.

In the Prelude to *Faust* Goethe writes:

> "Just such a drama let us now compose.
> Plunge boldly into life—its depths disclose!

Each lives it, not to many is it known
'Twill interest wheresoever seized and shown."

PSYCHOLOGICAL FREEDOM:—After what has been said about dogmatism in establishing the author's meaning of a piece of literature, we may seem to be plunging into a bold contradiction when we suggest the psychological elements in literature. But we are not asking or even suggesting that any one accept these findings. Indeed we will be pleased if you will doubt every statement in this book. Only be sure you find your own psychological life in the specific work. The suggestions are intended to stimulate a method of personal application.

We shall have occasion many times to say that such and such an author meant so and so. *All we mean to say is that he makes it possible for us to think so and so.*

SPECIFIC PSYCHOLOGICAL APPLICATIONS: —Up to this point the object has been to set forth the problems that must be met. I shall now proceed with specific illustrations in literature.

The genius is a condenser of human thought. When Rousseau cried out: "Man is born, lives, and dies in a state of slavery. At his birth he is wrapped in his swaddling clothes, at his death he is nailed in his coffin,"—he sums up volumes of the modern psychological tendency to extol environment.

The criminal has been and is destined to be a special study for modern psychology. In one brief sentence on *The Pale Criminal,* Nietzsche sums up the tendency of nearly every modern investigation—"'Enemy,' ye shall say, but not 'wicked one'; 'diseased one,' ye shall say, but not 'wretched'; 'fool,' ye shall say, but not 'sinner'."

Of all writers Shakespeare touched more aspects and details of human nature—which is psychology—than any other writer. His careful analyses of human acts abound on every page. His powerful imagination seems to have compelled creation—but creation that grasped life in every detail. Anger, jealousy, deceit, selfishness, hate, fear, superstition, hypocrisy, sympathy, friendship, love—all are weighed according to the situation.

G. Stanley Hall early gave attention to the psychology of jealousy. In *Othello* Iago presents a powerful description of its operation:

> "Trifles light as air
> Are to jealous conformations strong
> As proofs of holy writ."

Again in the same play we read:

> "Think'st on I'ld make of life a jealousy
> To follow still the changes of the moon
> With fresh suspicion?"

McDougall and others have recently demonstrated the large place which the instinct of *self-elation* plays in social life. Shakespeare sees its many degrees. He says:

> "The general's disdain'd
> By him one step below, he by the next,
> The next by him beneath; so every step,
> Expanded by the first pace that is sick
> Of his superiors, grows to an envious fever
> Of pale and bloodless emulation."

Ever since G. Stanley Hall awakened this country to an examination of the influence of the past and the pain which we experience in being dragged away from it, social psychology has given definite attention to this subject. Half of Ross's book *Social Psychology* is devoted to a discussion of superstition and tradition. Only follow briefly Ibsen's literary treatment of the subject in his tragedy—*The Master Builder*.[18] The Master Builder's beautiful home is burned down, resulting in the loss of the two little boys and everything they have. His wife laments not the loss of her boys, but of her ancient rugs and dolls.

Mrs. Solness. Oh, no, no, Miss Wangel—do not talk to me any more about the two little boys. We ought to feel nothing but joy in thinking of them; for they are so happy—so happy now. No, it is the small losses in life that cut one to the heart—the loss of all that other people look upon as almost nothing.

Hilda. (lays her arms on Mrs. Solness's knees, and looks up at her affectionately) Dear Mrs. Solness—tell me what things you mean!

Mrs. Solness. As I say, only little things. All the old portraits were burnt on the walls. And all the old silk dresses were burnt, that had belonged to the family for generations and generations. And all mother's and grand-mother's lace—that was burnt, too! And only think—the jewels, too! (Sadly) And then all the dolls.

Hilda. The dolls?

Mrs. Solness. (choking with tears) I had nine lovely dolls.

Hilda. And they were burnt too?

Mrs. Solness. All of them. Oh, it was hard—so hard for me.

Hilda. Had you put by all these dolls, then? Ever since you were little?

Mrs. Solness. I had not put them by. The dolls and I had gone on living together.

Hilda. After you were grown up?

Mrs. Solness. Yes, long after that.

Hilda. After you were married, too?

Mrs. Solness. Oh yes, indeed. So long as he did not see

it—. But they were all burnt up, poor things. No one thought of saving them. Oh, it is so miserable to think of. You musn't laugh at me, Miss Wangel.

Hilda. I am not laughing in the least.

Mrs. Solness. For you see, in a certain sense, there was life in them, too. I carried them under my heart—like little unborn children.

THE ALL-PERVADING PSYCHOLOGY:—Here we shall deal with three aspects of psychology which are more uncertain and indefinite than the examples just given.

First we have that over-powering something most akin to the spell produced by music. It is better felt than described. Let any one with maturity and experience listen to a grand opera or a symphony concert and attempt to describe his feelings and thoughts: he will soon find how inadequate words are. The reading of *Hamlet* leaves an indescribable feeling of admiration and disgust; a sense of weakness and a glimpse of one's possibilities. Ibsen's *Master Builder* and *Brand* inspire one to scale the heights to see the glories of the world.

Homer's *Iliad* brings to the front the three tragedies of human life—love, war, and religion. No great piece of literature has ever been written without play upon one or all of these tragedies.

These psychological effects are of supreme interest to the student of human nature. The art of teaching literature should aim to stimulate these effects to the limit. Indefinite as they may seem they are after all the deepest psychological aspects of human life. They lead to thinking, feeling, and new endeavor. In the subconscious the effect of such reading may exert an influence throughout life. Let the formalistic psychologist piece together his broken fragments of reflex arcs, synaptic connections and "squirmings." But he will never know human life unless these fragments be woven into one great whole.

In the second place we have the intellectual search for meanings as a whole. Is not the *Inferno* a figurative description of what goes on among the many instinctive conflicting emotions, feelings, desires, and ambitions of adolescence?

> "Midway upon our journey
> I found myself in a forest dark."

Does not Maeterlinck's *Blue Bird* represent man's fruitless search after happiness.

In any case the particular meaning is not the chief concern. But that the author has stimulated us to strive after *some meaning* is the chief psychological significance.

The third phase of any great piece of literature is the outstanding psychological principle, constantly suggested by the author: such as the psychology of crime, of custom, of suggestion, of human freedom, of heredity and environment, of instinct, of sex, of achievement, of symbolism, of the complexity of emotions, of sympathy, of deceit, of education, of the abnormal, of the subconscious. All these and others find expression in different pieces of literature.

Most of these psychological manifestations will receive special treatment later on. For example, in Galsworthy's *Justice* one learns the modern psychology of crime; in *The Pillars of Society,* deceit; in *Ghosts,* heredity; in *Pippa Passes,* the recent psychology of suggestion; in *Brand* and in *The Sorrows of Werther,* human freedom; in the *Divine Comedy* and *Hamlet,* complexity of emotions.

Some single pieces of literature contain many of these psychological principles. *Psychological symbolism dominates all great pieces of literature.* Two different methods of treatment are open to us: One consists in selecting a great piece of literature and attempting to summarize the psychological principles embodied in it. The other method consists in selecting specific psychological topics and then in selecting literary productions in which the given principle is manifested. We shall employ both methods.

CHAPTER VI

PSYCHOLOGICAL PRINCIPLES IN LITERATURE

IT IS SAFE to say that every phase of human life and conduct has appeared in literature to some extent. However some are more constant, dominant, and general than others. The emotional combinations have been more thoroughly explored and developed than have the intellectual. Again, recent literature has consciously and unconsciously introduced several distinctly modern tendencies in psychology, especially abnormal psychology. To appreciate the importance of literary psychology let us discuss briefly several of the different psychological aspects in literature. The remainder of the book will be devoted to the development of these topics. No effort will be here made to explain these topics because their explanation and application to life are developed in separate chapters. So the reader may look upon this outline as merely a suggestive guide to some of the different phases of human nature to be found in literature.

1. Psychological symbolism—Allegory.
2. Psychology of Achievement — Instinct of Self-elation—Biological Urge—Self-realization.
3. Psychological Suggestion—Modern Apperception.
4. Subtle Psychology in Literature—Sarcasm.
5. The Emotional Network—Complexes—Rationalization—Defense Mechanism.

6. Power of Custom—Tradition—Environment—Mind Set.
7. Heredity—Instinct—Destiny.
8. Psychological Freedom—Free will—Destiny—Responsibility—Human Freedom.
9. Psychology of Crime in Literature—The Modern Movement—Punishment.
10. Abnormal Psychology in Literature.
11. Recent Dominance of Social Psychology—Stimulation and Response—Group Action.
12. Sex Instinct—Sex complex.
13. Freudian Psychology—New Aspect of Sex.
14. The Pathos of Humanity—The Human Conflict.
15. Right and Wrong—Religion—Morals.
16. Psychology of Vengeance—Jealousy—Likes and Dislikes—War—Fear.
17. Marginal Consciousness—Subconsciousness—Unconsciousness.
18. Educational Reform.
19. Psychology of Religion.
20. Philosophy.

The findings of modern psychology on each of these topics have revolutionized human thinking on conduct. However, the best of literature long anticipated most of these lines of thinking. In many cases the agreement will be found to be outstanding and definite.

1. *Psychological Symbolism* has been almost entirely overlooked by the standard psychologists. Only Freud and his followers have given it consideration. In the *Interpretation of Dreams,* Freud holds that deep in the subconscious is hidden a dream material that is coherent and logical. The dream is the translation of this hieroglyphic material, or record of past life, into common speech. Im-

pressions in life, long past, are presented in symbolical form.

Attempts to analyze dreams scientifically were made in medicine and other fields long before Freud wrote his book on the *Interpretation of Dreams,* but it was he who gave us a new and elaborate method. Now all psychologists and medical men feel the significance of this theory, even if they do not accept it. Here we can neither defend the theory nor criticize it: we can only try to state the main features.

Freud holds that no mental activity is arbitrary or accidental. In the main, dreams must be considered as the result of suppressed and accumulated wishes. They also include the unconscious biological forces in us.

Again, Freud distinguishes between the dream content and the form of the dream in the same way in which we should distinguish between the form of a piece of literature and the real meaning underlying it. We must look for the real content of the dream in its symbolic nature. Like many stories and pieces of literature, the dream must be interpreted. Or, just as the best myths are now supposed to have had some meaning, purpose, or truth behind them, so it is with dreams.

Again, dreams are always dramatized—acted out. You are always in the action—*imaginary wish fulfilment*. Dreams contain the most intimate things of our life and nature. "Dreams," says Freud, "are the royal road to a knowledge of the unconscious in the soul."

Later we shall have occasion to discuss the subconscious in relation to literature. But here let us declare that there could be no literature without symbolism. It is equally difficult to see how psychological symbolism could have free play unless we assume a storehouse outside of consciousness. We do not hesitate to assume this force in the case of instinct, but in literature and intellectual activity we feel that it is mysticism.

However, symbolism began with the first use of language. Words are only signs or symbols and are open to a free play of the mind until convention fixes a meaning. One is naturally astonished that a work like "How We Think" makes so little use of psychological symbolism. It is equally surprising that the Gestalt Psychology developed by Koffka and Köhler, has not pushed further into the field of symbolism.

In primitive myths, stories, and literature psychological symbolism was the natural result of the free play of the mind, similar to that which Freud claims for dreams. Modern symbolism has become conscious of itself and is now a psychological art so well applied by writers as to produce what is known as the symbolist movement in literature. The birth of this movement witnessed the splendid funeral of literary formalism with its rules and its efforts to imitate the ancient world.

In the light of these psychological findings let us turn to literature for a fuller demonstration of this principle. We will accept the principle that *the greater a piece of literature the more varied, deeper, and far-reaching is the symbolism.*

Words are only symbols. But generally their symbolism has become so fixed that the reaction is fairly definite. So it is the unusual combination of words that produces literary symbolism. To this is added the cumulative effect of suggestion—indirect thinking. In literature we readily detect five forms of symbolism:

1. Symbolism of things.
2. Symbolism of events.
3. Symbolism of action or change.

4. Symbolism of characters.
5. Symbolism of the whole drama or work.

Since symbolism is the very heart of literature it is necessary to devote some space to each one of these.

1. Maeterlinck loves symbolism and some think that he has carried it to extremes—into the land of pure mysticism. He says: "Souls are weighed in silence." Maeterlinck pictures man as "a God who is afraid." In his *Blue Bird* we have the climax of symbolism—a host of characters most of which are used symbolically. Light represents intelligence; Darkness, ignorance and superstition; Oak Tree, age and strength.

Far-reaching and powerful symbolism is found in the thundering tragedies of Ibsen. In *The Pillars of Society,* ideas are embodied in symbols. Bernick is represented as one of the pretended Pillars of Society. He is so shrewdly corrupt that one thinks of the saying of Socrates: "Therefore we see that the most unjust of all men must appear to be the most just."

In this play Bernick has a fleet of ships. One of them is *The Indian Girl*. It is rotten, but Bernick has it covered over with paint. He orders her to sail for America even though his shipman tells him that she will go to the bottom of the sea. She carries relatives dangerous to the reputation of Bernick. But on the eve of sailing his only son runs away and hides on *The Indian Girl*.

In *An Enemy of the People* the scene is laid in a famous health resort. Dr. Stockmann discovers that the springs are drugged every night and that the people know it. He tells the people: "You'll poison the whole community in time." Then they rise up and stone him out of the town.

As already quoted from *The Master Builder* his house

is burned down and his two children lose their lives. The next day the mother is lamenting the loss, not of her children; "they are in heaven"; but "there were all my ancient rugs and my dolls—one—two—three—four—five—six—seven—eight—nine"—all burned up. The symbolism almost burns a hole in the paper.

Examine, if you will that puzzling combination of symbolisms, known as Dante's *Divine Comedy*.[19] It opens, proceeds, and closes with symbolism. When you read the opening lines:

"Mid-way upon our journey of life I found myself within a forest dark," you know that it is no ordinary journey and no real forest. And the closing lines:

"Even as a wheel that equally is moved,
   The love which moves the sun and the other stars"

are equally pregnant with meaning. Through Hell, Purgatory, and Paradise you move amidst one string of symbols.

The most important fact about literary symbolism is that it represents a deep psychological method of thinking—*the free and unlimited play of the mind and of self-expression.*

3. *To symbolize change and make it stand out as a reality is one of the highest and most difficult arts of literature.* From the time of Hereclitus to the modern functionalist psychologists this concept of *flux* or *constant change* as a reality has baffled psychological and philosophical minds. The functionalists have not succeeded in making clear to the average student the meaning of their position. In spite of all they say the "mind stuff" idea still persists. Action without conception of something that acts is no conception for small minds. The same difficulty has appeared in the modern efforts to conceive the end of action. Here we look forward with the same difficulty as

when looking backward. What is the end of action? *Action exists to beget more action.* Great literature has the advantage of permitting a variety of interpretations. Yet it requires great skill even to suggest this *flux idea.* Perhaps no other piece of literature accomplishes this idea in a higher degree than does Ibsen, in *Little Eyolf.*[20]

Allmers, the husband, has gone upon the mountain to write a book on *human responsibility.* Rita, the wife, is at home with Eyolf who was made a cripple by rolling off the table while the mother was busy with her own pleasure.

Allmers returns three weeks before he was expected. Asta, an aunt, has also arrived. She inquires about Allmers and says she had a strange feeling and that accounts for it. She asks if he has changed. Rita whispers: "He looked quite transformed as he stood in the doorway." She further says that he has not written a line of the book —"Only thinking and thinking and thinking."

But the supreme symbolism of change is the Rat-Wife who is now introduced. She carries a strange bag and while she is trying to bargain to clear the town of rats, Eyolf peeps in the bag and spies a dog. He wants to know if the dog bites the rats to death. She explains that the rats all follow her as she plays on her pan-pipes down to the shore. Then she gets in her boat but keeps on playing with one hand and the rats all follow her "out into the deep, deep sea."

The bargain is made. The family continues their reunion—all save Eyolf. After a while they begin to look for him, but find him nowhere. Allmers says something like a revolution has taken place within him. Asta tells him that he will never write the book. He replies: "But I will act out my human responsibility."

In a short while a cry is raised. People are rushing down to the sea and the cry is heard "the crutches are floating." Eyolf has followed the Rat-Wife into the sea. He lies at the bottom of the ocean with his accusing eyes looking up. Soon Rita and Allmers sit by the sea looking over the water—each accusing the other for Eyolf's being crippled and drowned.

One day Allmers comes to Rita as they sit by the sea. He says it is impossible for them to "forever keep circling around one fixed thought." Then Rita suggests that they take refuge in religion. He says: "Do you believe in Him? If you could follow Eyolf to where he is would you right now? Would you of your own free will leave every thing behind you? Renounce your earthly life?"

Rita says: "Today? This very hour? No, I think I should have to stay with you, a little while."

Then Allmers says: "But if I were over there too. Would you then—answer."

Rita says: "I should want to see you so much—but—I could not—I feel it. No, no, I never could for all the glory of heaven. I am too human. It is here that we living beings are at home."

Rita later builds an orphanage. Allmers suggests to his sister that the relation between brother and sister "is the only relation in life not subject to the law of change."

Here we are face to face with a keen analysis of human beliefs and a far-reaching mode of abstract thinking. But the play has its gripping effect even aside from these deep ideas.

CHAPTER VII

THE MEANING OF SYMBOLISM

WHILE WE ARE in the heart of our subject, let us consider two additional phases of symbolism in literature. It is only by viewing a subject from many angles that we arrive at a fair comprehension of the ideas involved.

1. *The symbolism of characters is one of the dominant features of literature.* These must in turn fit into the larger symbolism of the whole production. In teaching literature the suggestion as to the possible meaning of the characters should be presented from the beginning.

Unlike the symbolism of things this symbolism of characters can rarely be surmised from any single statement. Such conceptions are the result of an indefinite number of inferences and related ideas. However, psychological freedom stimulates such integration of inferences.

The following presentation must consist of some of the outstanding characters in literature with quotations to illustrate their meanings.

We can do no better than to begin with *Faust* and its short prologue in heaven.[21] Read the following and wherever reference is made to *Faust* read struggling humanity and for Mephistopheles the negative element that denies, and destroys.

Mephistopheles

"Of suns and worlds I have nothing to say,
I see alone mankind's self-torturing pains.

The little world-gold still the self-same stamp retains,
And is as wondrous now as on the primal day.
Better he might have fared, poor wight,
Hadst thou not given him a gleam of heavenly light;
Reason he names it and doth so
Use it than brutes more brutish still to grow.
With deference to your grace, he seems to me
Like any long-legged grasshopper to be,
Which ever flies, and flying springs,
And in the grass its ancient ditty sings.
Would he but always in the grass repose!
In every heap of dung he thrusts his nose. . . .
Men's wretchedness in sooth I so deplore,
Not even I would plague the sorry creatures more.

The Lord

Know'st thou my servant, Faust?

Mephistopheles

The doctor?

The Lord

Right.

Mephistopheles

He serves thee in strange fashion, as I think.
Poor fool! Not earthly is his food or drink.
An inward impulse hurries him afar,
Himself half conscious of his frenzied mood;
From heaven claimeth he its brightest star,
And from the earth craves every highest good,
And all that's near, and all that's far,
Fails to allay the tumult in his blood.

The Lord

Though now he serves me with imperfect sight,
I will ere long conduct him to the light.
The gardener knoweth, when the green appears,
That flowers and fruit will crown the coming years.

Mephistopheles

What wilt thou wager? Him thou yet shall lose,
If leave to me thou wilt but give,
Gently to lead him as I choose!

The Lord

So long as he on earth doth live,
So long 'tis not forbidden thee.
Man still must err, while he doth strive.

Mephistopheles

I thank you; for now willingly
I traffic with the dead, and still aver
That youth's plump blooming cheek I much prefer.
I'm not at home to corpses; 'tis my way,
Like cats with captive mice to toy and play."

With one great stroke Goethe transformed the objective devil into the evil selfish principle within the human heart as a natural part of human nature. Mephistopheles is the shrewd, intellectual, selfish nature of humanity that denies, destroys. The play opens with him a dominant character to whom Faust sells his soul and closes with him baffled and amazed as the Blessed Boys carry the soul of Faust to heaven.

Those who take only a narrow view of this tragedy are shocked at the idea that a woman must suffer and be executed to redeem a man. But the wider view sees

Margaret as the symbol of the *sufferings* the race must pass through on its dark road to redemption. As Helena in the second Part represents the spiritualistic phase of human development or the union of modernism with the good, true, and beautiful so does Margaret symbolize the physical and instinctive side of our development. But it is Margaret who receives the soul of Faust in heaven and asks to be his guide. The love passion is only an episode in the great drama.

That Faust represents humanity being led astray by the evil principle within us, struggling blindly to free itself, and its final redemption stands out in a hundred places. It is the pathos of the human struggle.

It is such far-reaching symbolism that lifts a piece of literature into the land of universality and furnishes food for thoughtful readers at the same time that it pleases by its imagery and its deep emotional tone.

In Dante's *Divine Comedy* we find all kinds of symbolism. But here we shall be concerned with only three outstanding characters. Dante or the *I* which dominates the whole of the drama stands for humanity, struggling with its avarice, its gluttony, its prodigality, its unsocial nature, its malice, its violence against people and property, its immorality, its hypocrisy, its deception, its thievery.

Who or what can deliver man from the forest dark? Only Virgil—the symbol of reason and human intelligence. Hundreds of passages may be found to justify this symbolism, but only a few definite ones are needed. As we pass through the hell and ascend into purgatory, Virgil more and more definitely reveals his need and mission. As they approach heaven some guide besides intelligence must be found. Here you are face to face with the dispute of his time over rationalism versus inspiration —divine insight.

If you have any doubt, listen to these lines:

"And unto me Virgilius said: 'My son,
   Here may indeed be torment, but not death.
Remember thee, remember! and if I
   On Geryon have safely guided thee,
   What shall I do now I am nearer God?
Believe for certain, shouldst thou stand a full
   Millennium in the bosom of this flame,
   It could not make thee bald a single hair.
And if perchance thou think that I deceive thee,
   Draw near to it, and put it to thy proof
   With thine own hands upon thy garment's hem.
And lay aside, now lay aside all fear,
   Turn hitherward, and onward come securely,'
   And I stood motionless, and 'gainst my conscience!
Seeing me stand still motionless and stubborn,
   Somewhat disturbed he said: "Now look thou, Son
   'Twixt Beatrice and thee there is this wall."

Dante's dead sweetheart—Beatrice, now becomes his guide. Do we need anything more to realize that Beatrice symbolizes divine insight into things that lie beyond human intelligence?

As she reveals herself to Dante she says:

Continued she, like unto one who speaks,
   And keeps his warmest utterance in reserve:
"Look at me well; in sooth I'm Beatrice!
   How didst thou deign to come unto the Mountain?
   Didst thou not know that man is happy here?"

In Tolstoy's *War and Peace* Napoleon stands not only for the general who commanded 600,000 men to march into Russia, but also for selfish ambition that wrecks humanity. The two families of Rostoffs and Balkonskys represent two distinct kinds of civilization; the first represents a civilization gone to seed and decaying; the Balkonskys are symbolic of a new order dominated by simplicity and honesty.

In Moliere's masterpiece—*Misanthrope*—Philinte is the embodiment of a society given over to hypocrisy, frivolity and villainy. Philinte says: "I look upon all these faults of which you complain as vices inseparably connected with human nature; in short my mind is no more shocked at seeing a man a rogue, unjust or selfish, than at seeing vultures eager for prey."

Ibsen makes it possible to symbolize almost every one of his characters. In spite of his reported protest against it the urge is there. In creating this urge he has achieved a universal and lasting literary form which will remain an attraction to thoughtful readers.

Those who see only the pessimistic outlook of Ibsen overlook the fact that he, like Tolstoy, everywhere indicates that society is only crusted over with false forms, religion, and superstition. Underneath the superficial life of *Nora,* in "The Doll's House," slumbers a strong personality and character.

In like manner we find that Bernick—this corrupt society—wakes up:

"Where have I been?" he exclaims. "You will be horrified when you know. Now, I feel as if I had just recovered my senses after being poisoned. But I feel—I feel that I *can* be young and strong again."

Note the words: "I feel that I *can* be young and strong again."

Ibsen's last work—"When We Dead Awake"—has puzzled students. Many dismiss it as the product of a decaying mind. Few will agree with me in my ideas of its far-reaching symbolism. But this does not matter. I am not trying to agree or disagree with anyone. I am trying to show the significance of a fundamental form of thinking.

Many things urge to the conviction that *We Dead* symbolizes this same society about which he had long written —as well as himself. Here is in brief the story. Rubek, a sculptor of many years renown, and his young wife Maia are seated at the table in a fashionable summer resort. Silence reigns. Maia says: "Don't you hear the stillness?" It develops that they are quite unsuited to each other. In a few minutes a Bear Hunter enters. Maia goes out to see his dogs. In a few minutes Maia returns to announce that she is going up the mountain with the Bear Hunter. She tells Rubek that he has promised to take her up on the mountain and show her all the glories of the world and that he has never done it.

At the same time a strange woman has taken her seat at the table. Maia tells Rubek that she is probably one of the many models he has had. He says he has never had but one.

Maia is off. Rubek recognizes the newcomer as Irene, his former model. She tells him that she has been dead many years. Rubek wanted to know why she left him. He charges her with stealing the keys to his tool chest and says he has been able to do nothing since.

She in turn charges him that he promised to take her upon the mountain and show her all the glories of the world. She tells him that he was too inhuman. Then for some pages we are led to believe that a real child is theirs. *Irene* says:

> "I went into the darkness—
> When the child stood transfigured in the light."

Rubek tells Irene that he has waited for her year after year—without knowing it. Irene tells him that she could not come to him, that she was lying down in the grave, that she has now risen, but not transfigured. Rubek promises to take her upon the mountain and show her all the glory of the world. So at the appointed time they are off to spend a night on the upland.

They pass up the mountain and meet Maia and the Bear Hunter coming down.

Soon a great thunder-like sound is heard and whirling snow comes down the mountain; as Maia's voice is heard in the valley, singing: "I am free, I am free!"

For any one who knows the literary struggle of Ibsen there is an irresistible feeling that it means his own struggle between Realism and Idealism. In his early life Irene—Idealism—was his only model. Then he turned to Realism—married Maia. In the later part of his life he is reunited to Irene and wrote his three great works:—"Little Eyolf," "The Master Builder" and "When We Dead Awake."

We have already emphasized the fact that symbolism is an unconscious primitive method of thinking. Since the Greeks did not make any sharp distinction between the natural and supernatural, the gods could readily symbolize the forces of nature. Apparently Zeus was a symbol for that Fate or Destiny which played such a large part in their thinking. Characters have been used as symbols in many ancient myths.

CHAPTER VIII

SYMBOLIC SIGNIFICANCE OF THE WHOLE

THE VARIATIONS OF symbolism in literature are as infinitely multiple as are modes of human thinking. In some pieces of literature the significance of the combined symbolism stands out. In others no such unification is urged upon you. No effort should be made to construct larger meanings where repeated suggestions do not beckon. The first part of *Faust* takes on an entirely different meaning when viewed in its larger significance. Dante's *Divine Comedy,* if viewed in only one of its three parts, has a meaning radically different from that of the whole. The symbolism may deal with social, political, or religious problems. The significance of Galsworthy's *Justice* cannot be confined to the sympathy and pity excited for Folders and Honeywill. It involves the whole social order and the causes of human conduct.

In considering that pleasing, bewildering combination of symbolism found in Maeterlinck's *Blue Bird.* Most writers agree that the theme is the *human search for happiness.* But the outcome of this search depends largely upon the reader's personal psychology or mind set. A half dozen or more answers are suggested. Two children—Tyltyl and Mytyl—are given a magic diamond and sent out to find *The Blue Bird.*

They journey into the Land of Memories overhung by a dense fog. Finally they are in conversation with their dead brothers and sisters, granddaddy and grandmamma. The Blue Bird is caught but turns black in the light.

Granddaddy tells them that of course we always live—in your memories.

They next journey into the Palace of Night. They enter the rooms of sicknesses, evils, misfortunes, Ghosts, Wars, and Perfumes. In the last they get great numbers of Blue Birds; but their wings soon droop and they die. It is most significant that Light—Intelligence—refuses to enter the Palace of Night.

They explore the Forest which is most complicated. Everything rebels against having their secrets exposed. Light says it is always so. It all ends in rebellion in which the dog and Tyltyl are injured. No Blue Birds are found.

Act Four is devoted to a search in the Enchanted Palace of all men's joys and happiness. This Palace is in charge of Fate. Light dare not enter. The joys cannot endure here. When the Diamond is turned the Luxuries escape into the gallery of the Miserable. Even in the gallery of Maternal Love, Mytyl observes that the mothers are all in tears.

The company, except Fire, search the Graveyard. They think that some one is hiding the Blue Bird behind a tombstone. The dead arise. It is a most terrifying scene, but no Blue Birds are found.

Finally they explore the Kingdom of the Future. Here everything is blue. Even the children that are yet to be born are blue. They see all the children yet to be born and some strange creatures said to be coming after man. Father Time—Fate—has absolute control. They go only when he says and the clock strikes. Only no one can come to earth empty handed. He must have some new *social remedy, new disease, calamity,* a *new crime*. Father Time does not care, but they must have something.

In it adult psychology is adapted to the child mind. We have a long list of suggestions of possible meanings. It has consistency and unity in its suggestions and symbolisms. I have selected it because of its many possible psychological meanings.

1. It may raise the question whether happiness exists at all. The Blue Bird symbolizes happiness. But it seems not to exist at all. Only Tyltyl's faint blue bird existed and it flew away when he gave it to another.

2. Again, it may mean that happiness escapes us when we pursue it. Only when we accept conditions as they are and cease to strive to change them is happiness found. The children had it at home and did not realize it.

3. Also there are many suggestions that Light, or Intelligence, is dangerous to happiness.

4. Happiness is relative. Many suggestions support this idea. The Blue Birds that change, the closing words of Light, the happiness of the mothers—all indicate that we look for something that is only a comparison. In short, happiness is in our mode of thinking.

5. That fate or heredity controls our destiny is strongly suggested in The Kingdom of the Future.

6. We also have the suggestion that happiness lies in the imaginative future. This thoroughly agrees with James Branch Cabell, in his *Beyond Life*. There he maintains that after childhood the average individual is unable to face reality. The Demi-Urge to Romance leads to the creation of all kinds of future worlds. Religion is the greatest romance ever created by man.

I have selected this play because it is simple, yet it contains suggestions for many possible interpretations. Which one shall we accept? It is up to the reader. It is not the specific result that matters, but the method or psychological bent of mind.

Ibsen's *Brand* is among the great pieces of world literature. For symbolism as a whole it is in a class with *Faust,* the *Divine Comedy,* and a few others. It is only by putting

together a great string of symbolisms that we arrive at
the large conception of the whole.

Brand is a man of iron will. He acts the part of a
priest but refuses to be called one. He says: "Scarce know
if I'm a Christian." He is first seen high on a foggy
mountain. Near by stands two lovers—Agnes and Einer.
They are singing a song: "We are going to get married
and live happy a hundred years and then off to heaven."
Brand shouts out to them to be careful because there is a
great chasm in front of them and the fog is thick on the
mountain. Brand starts down the mountain and the
strange character—Gerd cries out to him:

> Come with me, you; and I will show
> A church built out of ice and snow.

Some hours later Brand, Agnes, and Einar are down by
the sea. They are all sheltered from the fearful storm, in
a little shack. Out of the wild stormy night a woman
rushes in calling for a priest. Since that is Einer's determined mission in life, Agnes bids him go. But he will
not brave the storm. Brand offers his service, but says
some one must row the boat. When no one else offers
Agnes puts on her coat and goes.

Days later Brand asked Agnes to be his wife. But
before he let her answer he warned her that he demanded
all or nothing. She bowed to it and this doctrine dominates the whole play. One disaster after another follows
in the application of it. Brand's mother seeks a confer-
ence with him and asks that he come to her death bed.
He replies that she had stolen all his father had and that
she must give up *all or nothing*. She offers three fourths
and still he refuses.

Three years later Brand is serving the people in a low
swampy town. Agnes reads anxiety in his silent look. He

tells her that he is expecting a message from his mother. Agnes tells him that, if she is graveward bound, he should go without a message, that he is hard, that many a soul has fallen away before his watchword of *All or Nothing*.

Brand looks into the room where little Alf is slumbering. As he turns away he reels with dizziness. Agnes trembles as she sees him. He says God is good and will not take away their joy.

Just then the Doctor passes by to tell him that his mother is very low and that he should not be so hard.

Brand goes into the house; Agnes peeps through the open door and says:

> "He kneels beside his darling child,—
> As if with sobs, he rocks his head,
> And presses close against the bed
> As one whom helpless woe makes wild.—
> O what a wealth of love this strong."

The Doctor now urges him to leave if he wishes to save the life of Alf. He says: "Pack, and go hence, for Heaven's sake!" Brand replies: "Not though the earth beneath me shake!" "Stay then," says the Doctor, "and doom your child to death." Then the Doctor upbraids him for wavering in his doctrine of *All or Nothing* when it becomes personal and *Gerd* appears to point a finger of scorn at Brand and again invites him to her ice church.

In the midst of indescribable agony Brand turns to Agnes. She says: "Ask thy God—Go where He saith." Agnes has the child in her arms as she stands in the door. Brand would put the choice on her. She points to the garden gate. Brand says: "No, here!" Brand clasps his hands to his heart, bursts into tears and throws himself down on the steps crying: "Jesus, give me light!" Soon little Alf is laid to rest on the knoll near the house.

Now it is Christmas Eve. Agnes is waiting for Brand to come and looking at all the things that used to be Alf's. She has a tree and a candle shining out on the grave. Brand returns, forbids her tears and revival of past memories. Yet she detects that he himself has been crying and is in a cold sweat. He tries to say it is the spray from the sea.

Brand would explain that all is for the best and the child is now in heaven.

Agnes finally dies of silent grief.

Einar appears to upbraid Brand and accuse him of killing Agnes. The Sheriff and the Dean of the Church appear to make Brand turn everything into show and display— Politics—State Church. The church is completed. But Brand tells them that the church will never be opened; that he has only given up a small lie for a bigger one. The crowd follows Brand off into the wilderness and up the mountain. They become hungry, weary, and dissatisfied. The Sheriff and the Dean follow and persuade them to return. Brand struggles on up the mountain. He covers his face with his hands and throws himself down on the snow.

Brand (bursts into quiet tears)

> Alf and Agnes! O come back!
> Where the peaks are bleak and black,
> Lone I sit, the winds blow through me,
> Chilled by visions weary and gloomy—

Through the mist he sees the form of a woman—it is Agnes. She asks him to haste and come with her—Alf still lives. She tells him that he must erase three words—All or Naught—from memory pages.

Plato's Allegory of the Cave [22] is one of the greatest

philosophical and psychological allegories ever created by man. By a winding road he has a man leave the sunlight of heaven and enter an underground cave. Soon he encounters a fire. In front of the fire is a wall as high as a man. Between the wall and the fire are men walking and carrying all manner of objects on their heads. The shadows of these images are cast on the great natural back wall of the cave. On the other side of the wall he finds human beings chained to the wall. They are watching the images come and go. They all know in advance of time what images will appear next and how they will look. *There is not even any room for difference of opinion.*

He cuts the chains of one of them and drags him out of the cave. When he is out he is blind. But by and by he can see by the light of the stars, then the moon, then by the light of the sun, and finally he can look at the sun.

He *willingly* goes back and takes his place in the cave. But he begins to tell different stories about the images that come and go. The chained men call him crazy and rebel against any others being taken out of the cave. Aside from any consideration of Plato's doctrine of ideas, what a tragic symbol of the psychological struggle of human thought! One is immediately reminded of Francis Bacon's four idols that stand in the way of the advancement of learning.

The triple division of mind into Intellect, Feeling, and Will dates back to Plato's description of the Driver driving two horses up a high mountain on which is located valuable treasures. The road is steep and slopes down the hill. The driver must manage two antagonistic horses. One strives toward the top of the mountain; the other pulls downward. The driver is Will. The upper horse is Intellect, and the unruly horse is the Emotions. This division of the human soul held sway in theology and psychology for more than a thousand years. Indeed it has never been eradicated from theology, and in spite of modern science this division still remains for some psychologists. It dominates the *Divine Comedy*. The *will-idea* is dominant in most of Ibsen's writings. Yet such a great physician as Dr. Lorand tells us that will always mean healthy thyroid, adrenal and sexual glands. Certainly these examples should be proof of the struggle of literature to explore the mystery of human conduct. In many cases natural insight has discerned what subsequent scientific inquiry confirms.

One more facet of symbolism as a whole will suffice for our purposes. This we take from the vast field of psychological stories. We have already had a glimpse of this method in the chapter on *Psychology in Stories*. Tolstoy, Olive Schreiner and others made constant use of it; so did Poe and Hawthorne.

The Cherry Orchard [23] was first produced in Moscow in 1904. In the same year the author died at the early age of 44. The cherry orchard symbolizes decaying Russia. The events in Russia in the last few years make the play seem like a prophecy.

The cherry orchard is weighed down with one mortgage after another until the interest cannot be paid. A great landowner and merchant manipulates everything. The orchard is advertised for sale. It is sold to the merchant and landowner who proceeds to tear down the mansion and chop down the cherry orchard.

From beginning to end this play is one powerful procession of symbols. Madame Ranevsky is the owner of the cherry orchard — conservative Russia mortgaged down with superstition and tradition, with an artificial existence, tied up with intrigues of all kinds. *Anya,* her daughter of seventeen, represents hopeful youth—new society—young Russia. Trophinof is the world student, looking for wise and happy reforms, yet not anticipating any great immediate results.

Madame Ranevsky

" 'Oh, the sins that I have committed—I've always squandered money at random like a madwoman; I married a man who made nothing but debts. My husband drank himself to death on champagne; he was a fearful drinker. Then for my sins I fell in love and went off with another man; and immediately—that was my first punishment—a blow full on the head . . . here, in this very river . . . my little boy was drowned; and I went abroad, right, right away, never to come back any more, never to see this river again . . . I shut my eyes and ran, like a mad thing, and he came after me, pitiless and cruel. I bought a villa at Mentone, because he fell ill there, and for three years I knew not rest day or night; the sick man tormented and wore down my soul.

Trophimof

All Russia is our garden. The earth is great and beautiful; it is full of wonderful places. (A pause.) Think, Anya, your grandfather, your great-grandfather and all your ancestors were serf-owners, owners of living souls. Do not human spirits look out at you from every tree in the orchard, from every leaf and every stem? Do you not hear human voices? . . . Oh! It is terrible. Your orchard frightens me. When I walk through it in evening or at night, the rugged bark on the trees glows with dim light, and the cherry-trees seem to see all that happened a hundred and two hundred years ago in painful and oppressive dreams. Well, well, we have fallen at least two hundred years behind the times. We have achieved nothing at all as yet; we have not made up our minds how we stand with the past; we only philosophize, complain of boredom, or drink vodka. It is so plain that, before we can live in the present, we must first redeem the past, and have done with it; and it is only by suffering that we can redeem it, only by strenuous, unremitting toil. Understand that, Anya.

Anya

The house we live in has long since ceased to be our house; and I shall go away, I give you my word.

Trophimof

If you have the household keys, throw them in the well and go away. Be free, be free as the wind."

The whole play symbolizes the transition in Russia. It is the masterpiece of Chekhov.

This rather lengthy presentation of symbolism has been necessary. Symbolism is a primitive as well as modern mode of thinking. No consideration of how we think is complete without it. Besides this nearly all the psychological phases of conduct we shall present are hidden under some form of symbolism. The unification of knowledge indicates the highest type of mind. Philosophy is completely unified knowledge, says Spencer.

CHAPTER IX

PSYCHOLOGY OF ACHIEVEMENT
IN LITERATURE

MODERN PSYCHOLOGY IS filled with works on the will to power, on the self-elation instinct; on biological desires, impulses and urges. We have many investigations on success and ambition. The deterministic power of early impressions, as found in Freudian psychology, have been offered as an explanation of genius. History is one great exhibition of these biological and psychological forces. On them we have many and conflicting views. But nowhere do we have proper consideration of what literature and men of literary insight have left us on these topics.

The biological tendencies are soon linked with conscious ambition, desire for leadership, money-, and power-getting. Finally they form the only explanation for psychological delusions. They aid in our great struggle to escape reality, to create a new heaven and a new earth.

The universal appeal of literature is mainly due to the fact that it feeds these natural, biological impulses, the great hungers of humanity. They lie too deep for scientific psychology. These forces do not readily lend themselves to graphs, curves, and mathematical treatment. Literature is the only human device that has yet given any fair account of this phase of humanity. In much of shallow modern literature the treatment is open to serious criticism, due to the half digested biology and psychology that has been forced into recent literature. But that is not true of great literature of either ancient or modern times. Philosophy has often undertaken the task, but it has usually wound up so far away from human life as to be almost entirely ineffective.

Again, conflicts of these urges with other impulses and with external conditions form the background of all the tragedies of human life. Volumes would be needed to trace this development in literature. We can only touch the high points.

FORMS OF MANIFESTATION. The achievement impulse may appear as an intellectual mystery such as we find in the tragedy of Job, or in the attitude of the Hindus who said: "Something compels me somewhere; yet I see no meaning in life's long mystery." It may appear in great epics such as *The Mahabharata* of India; Homer's *Iliad* or *Odyssey; The Death of Seigfried,* or *Paradise Lost.* Its modern biological form exists in hundreds of social reform works like *A Far Country, The Weavers, The Sunken Bell, Anna Christie, The Escape, Justice, Man and Superman, The Cherry Orchard, Les Miserables.* Its more religious and philosophical aspects are developed by such great works as we have already suggested: *Faust, Brand, The Divine Comedy, Thus Spake Zarathustra, The City of God, The Republic, The Interlude,* and *Beyond Life* by James Branch Cabell.

Hundreds of works have emphasized the eternal conflict of the self-elation urges, but in this field none can be compared to Shakespeare. Conflicting psychological tendencies and emotions dominate all his plays as they do life. Ibsen, on the other hand, not only brings human urges into conflict, but looks ahead to the future social and philosophical significance and outcome.

In a proper study of psychology, our only concern should be to ask objectively in how far such and such views or principles are true to life. For this purpose a large view of the universal struggle of the race from savagery to modern civilization is necessary. The question is whether literature and the sociological history of humanity meet.

NIETZSCHE AND ACHIEVEMENT. The universal hunger for achievement, for change, for a new world may assume a variety of forms. For Nietzsche it became purely an intellectual struggle. Everything must be sacrificed to this development. He reduced good and happiness to an intellectual achievement. "What is good? Whatever augments the feeling of power, the will to power, power itself, in man. What is happiness?—the feeling that power increases—that resistance is overcome." Nietzsche looked on the instinct for growth, for survival, for the accumulation of force, for *power* as the core of evolution. He says: "I teach you beyond man. Ye have made your way from worm to man and much within you is still worm. Once ye were apes; even now man is ape in a higher degree than any ape."

Even in his dissertation on War and Warriors he says: "Let your love unto life be your love unto your highest hope; and your highest hope the highest thought of your life." Concerning the 1001 goals which Zarathustra found in many lands all were values created by man. But their dominant defect was that of *resignation*. The great psychological and philosophical scholar Davidson described the Middle Ages as being due to the hypnotic effect of a universal inferiority complex. The creation of a goal-made humanity.

In his brief topic—*The Way of the Creator*—Zarathustra says: "Thou must be ready to burn thyself in thine own flame: how canst thou become new, if thou hast not first become ashes?" Nietzsche's intellectual war, his road to power, is made clear when he has Zarathustra bid farewell to his dead companion and choose as living companions the *serpent* and the *eagle*—symbols of learning, intelligence, and courage.

Now have we here a psychology wholly wrong or only lopsided? Its foundation is certainly built on nature. The whole of it doubtless contains more truth than most of us are willing to acknowledge. It is very common for us to recognize inwardly more truth than we are willing to confess, even to ourselves. This is the main psychological explanation of the universal appeal of *The Rubaiyat*. However I think that our chapter on Psychology in Stories has furnished sufficient evidence that Nietzsche's intellectual achievement is only one side of human development. The idea carried to extremes would give us a world of Iagos such as Shakespeare pictures in *Othello*— men with intellect, cunning, and desire for vengeance, but with nothing to balance them. I cannot admit that conditions or teachings are responsible for sympathy, pity, and emotional evolution. These have a biological background as well. On the other hand we must admit that the various goals of humanity have been first determined by the leaders, often for their own benefit and will to power.

Let us turn to a world-famed drama for a wider view of the Psychology of Achievement. *Faust* represents the evolution of a soul through all the circumstances and relations of life. At the same time the author suggests the evolution of humanity and its ultimate destiny. The struggling soul of *Faust* reflects humanity. Faust makes many mistakes, but his unity of purpose and his persistent effort overcome all obstacles and lead ultimately to the great achievement—*truth*.

We may disagree somewhat in applying this great symbolic drama, but all careful students will agree that it is a masterly conception of the struggles, development, blunders, and ultimate redemption of man. That there is any such golden age ahead for humanity may be open to question; but that humanity seeks it no one can doubt.

We have seen how Dante's *Divine Comedy* represents

life's struggle, and how Ibsen's works—especially *Brand* —drives this idea home. It is present in hundreds of other works. Bojer's *Great Hunger* is one of the best modern representations of the power of these biological urges. These people may not have studied biology and psychology, but they saw life in its elemental aspect. Especially have such idealistic and philosophic poets as Browning and Longfellow busied themselves with this achieving impulse.

In his poem on *Andrea del Sarto,* Browning shows how disappointed the artist was over the title so often applied to him, of the "faultless painter." He exclaims: "Ah, but a man's reach shall exceed his grasp, or what's a heaven for?" In *The Last Ride Together,* Browning not only makes a rejected lover take refuge in the thought that if he had won he would have had nothing to spur him on, but he makes him recount all worthy achievements of great souls and realize that their reach exceeded their grasp.

When the world-renowned Danish sculptor unveiled his statue of Christ, loud were the praises and congratulations of his friends; but in the midst of it all he was found weeping. "My genius is decaying," he cried. "What do you mean?" they asked. "This statue," he answered, "is the first of my works that has completely satisfied me. 'Til now my ideals have been far beyond what I could execute, but it is so no longer. I can never create a great work again."

There are two other aspects of this psychology of achievement in literature which claim our attention—the conflict of these biological urges, and the social achievement literature.

CONFLICTING URGES. The conflict of impulses, instincts, desires and achievements is absolutely necessary for tragedy as generally understood. It is true that

Chekhov, the Russian writer, attempted to show that the slow wasting away of lives is unconscious suicide and as tragic as murder. It may be objective tragedy, but it is not subjective tragedy.

Shakespeare's tragedies are conflicts. We look in vain for anything tragic in Iago, for he is devoid of inner struggle: he is not comparable to the divided soul of *Othello,* which excites in the reader the most intense fear and pity—the two chief psychological elements in tragedy. We witness in the soul of Othello the awful conflict between the biological instincts of *love* and *jealousy*..

Read the following description of Othello's agony. Scene II (a bedchamber in the castle. Desdemona in bed, asleep)

Enter *Othello* with a light.

Othello. It is the cause, it is the cause, my soul—
    Let me not name it to you, you chaste stars!
    It is the cause. Yet I'll not shed her blood;
    Nor scar that whiter skin of hers than snow,
    And smooth as monumental alabaster.
    Yet she must die, else she'll betray more men.
    Put out the light, and then put out thy light:
    If I quench thee, thou flaming minister,
    I can again thy flaming light restore,
    Should I repent me; but, once put out thy light,
    Thou cunning'st pattern of excelling nature,
    I know not where is that Promethean heat
    That can thy light resume. When I have pluck'd the rose,
    I cannot give it vital growth again,
    It needs must wither; I'll smell it on the tree.
    (Kisses her)
    Ah, balmy breath, that does almost persuade
    Justice to break her sword! One more, one more:

Be thus when thou art dead, and I will kill thee,
And love thee after. One more, and that's the last:
So sweet was ne'er so fatal. I must weep,
But they are cruel tears: this sorrow's heavenly;
It strikes where it doth love. She wakes."

One may search literature in vain to find a better description of the conflict of ambition and achievement than that in the third act of *Hamlet*. The whole play is representative of this eternal conflict in human life.[24]

In 400 B. C. Euripides was a modern writer, to be classed with Ibsen and Strindberg. He saw the biological and psychological nature of man in its true nakedness. His works tally with modern psychology. He saw the dangers of sex suppression. He realized the power of instinctive achievement. In *Electra* he depicts a struggle towards a rational and human basis for all morality.

In ancient Hindu literature we encounter everywhere the struggle between the idealistic achievement and the biological urges of humanity.[25]

SOCIAL ACHIEVEMENT CONFLICTS. This conflict is the very heart of realistic drama. Molière, in his comic dramas, maintains a determined criticism of tradition, superstition, and hypocrisy. His *Would-be Gentleman* is a ridicule of the education of his time. He also saw clearly the conflict between reason and emotion.

The psychological struggle for achievement may be individual, centering about deep-seated natural impulses or determined by external conditions. In the social drama the struggle usually takes place between groups or masses.

In Ibsen's *Rosmersholm* the struggle is to bring himself in harmony with the urge "to work"—*to harmonize his actions with his convictions*. He penetrates to the depths of *moral consciousness* and shows its semi-conscious power rooted in ancient traditions. In this drama

Rebekka West's vision, insight, purpose, and character point to the far-reaching future, yet she stands under the shadow of the past.

The Lady From the Sea is Ibsen's chief evolutionary drama. He seems to have grasped the psychological idea expressed by G. Stanley Hall, that all the forces of nature have a lasting effect upon the human soul. Ellida Wangel struggles against the deep-seated forces of nature. The sea exercises over people a mood which works like a will. The sea can hypnotize. The great mystery is man's dependence upon the "will-less."

The conflict of group with group in the struggle for achievement is manifested in most forms of modern literature. Sudermann presents the conflict of the new generation with stabilized conservatism. Many novels and social dramas dive into the psychology of the struggle between aristocracy and democracy.

The Weavers, by Hauptmann,[26] will furnish an illustration of these efforts. For the hero we have a mob— The Weavers. It is the weavers as a class that stand out. A few characters are developed but not enough to center attention on them. The reader is in no way urged to be interested in one side or the other.

This is one of the earliest dramas bearing directly on the social conflict. The interest is centered in the struggle. There are speakers for and against capitalists. Some hold that things should not be forced, that many weavers have climbed to wealth and independence. On the other hand the weavers become rebellious and ready for any desperate thing. Another says that "before the weaver has a bed you get his coffin ready. You know before the doctor when death is on the way to knock at your door."

No better example of mob psychology can be found and how transformations take place. The weavers say: "We must help ourselves." Old Baumert says: "But as soon as we got the first good bite inside us we're different men. Damn it all! You feel the power comin' into you 'til you're like an ox an' that wild with strength that you hit out right and left without as much as takin' time to look. One, two, three, an' we're inside the house. Then at it like lightning—bang, crack." Another suggests that it would not be bad to start a little fire. He says more and more will soon be joining us.

CONCLUSION. Here the search for the psychology of achievement in literature must end. If the findings of literature have been sometimes inadequate and sometimes exaggerated, they are, nevertheless, in harmony with biological psychology. These findings form an endless supplement to such books as *The Will To Believe,* by James, and McDougall's *Social Psychology.*

The contention of many readers may be that these writers are only a few extremists, that the masses of humanity are not dominated by achievement tendencies. While the masses may not have the particular objectives that our presentation has brought to the front, yet the vast majority are urged on to some objective—heaven probably being the most common one. This is only one form of ideal existence: it is always pictured as an improvement over present conditions. It is one form of the urge to escape the present struggle—a manifestation of the self-elation instinct—or Cabell's Demi-Urge to Romance.

Again let it be remembered that literature has an appeal only in proportion as it reveals yourself to yourself—as it seems to be an extension of yourself. The foundation for this appeal must be in humanity. Biography and literature appeal to us in proportion as they reveal hidden possibilities of achievement or of suffering. Human life is everywhere a struggle for achievement. It may be largely blind, instinctive, and impulsive, or it may be guided by some degree of enlightenment. In collective and social life strife would cease to exist if these biological urges did not exist.

External conditions, calamities of nature, and death produce some degree of limitation and absolute dependence. Thus life takes on its tragic nature. This sense of limitation, of dependence, found its most sublime expression in the "Book of Job." Job's problem is the same problem of the destiny of man which we have encountered a dozen times in this chapter. His sincerity, his simplicity, his sublime sadness, and his reconciliation have never been equalled—so true are they to the heart of man.

CHAPTER X

COMPLEXITY OF EMOTIONS IN LITERATURE

MODERN PSYCHOLOGY HAS made less progress in the study of the complex emotional life than in any other field. The interrelationship of the emotions has been a subject of much dispute, and the theories of the emotions are far from being settled now.

What mature individual has never been tossed to and fro by anger, remorse, shame, love, jealousy or hatred? Well does Goethe make Werther exclaim: "What a thing is the heart of man! It is the sole source of everything—of our strength, happiness and misery." Many a psychologist is prematurely old and his heart is a burned out cinder. What does the average psychologist know of hate that makes men mad and bestial, of love that is blind and uncalculating, but still stronger than life itself; of fear that paralyzes and makes the blood run cold and slow; of courage that faces death in the crudest forms; of pleasurable pain—the *luxury of grief*. When the psychologist deals with these his heart is too often bankrupt and his knowledge bookish and empty words.

Men may wilfully torture their bodies or rejoice in torture by others. Only read James's chapter on the *Sin-Sick Soul*. He says: "The normal process of life contains moments as bad as any of those with which insane melancholy is filled. . . . The lunatic's visions of horror are all drawn from the material of daily fact. . . . If you protest, my friend, wait until you arrive there yourself." [27]

Bruno is imprisoned for many years; finally he is bound to the stake, surrounded by the multitude of scoffers and onlookers; his priestly accusers wish some excuse to let him go, and when they ask him if he has anything to say, with scorn for them and rejoicing in his persecution, he replies, "I foresee that you dread this more than I do."

We shall never understand literature until we get at least a glimpse of this side of life. Homer represents one of his characters as "rejoicing in his tears." The attraction of a work like the *Rubaiyat* may be ascribed to a sweet philosophical sorrow that has no kinship to misery or distress. With sorrowful pleasure our minds play about the unanswerable questions of life.

The feelings are fundamental, whereas the intellect is a secondary product. The chief business of the intellect is to devise ways and means to satisfy the deep longings of the human heart. The impetus to great undertakings is given not by the intellect, but by the feelings. Strong desire, love, anger, fear, vengeance, ambition inspire men with ideas. History demonstrates that the chief force of civilization resides in the feelings.

When you find a man defending a given policy or line of conduct, do not look at his logic but search diligently for what he feels to be his interest. In most cases the facts accepted or rejected, as well as his logic, are governed by it. I do not mean that he is a hypocrite, but deep desire makes straight for its object and focuses the intellect in one definite direction. Nor does this apply to the achievement of selfish ends only. It applies with equal force to the moral reformer. Here for the feeling of personal interest is substituted the feeling of duty or obligation. As viewed in after years the short-sightedness of most moral reformers is incomprehensible to the historian who seeks for logical reasons. Quietly and passively the historian reasons at his desk, whereas the doers of these deeds reasoned from an inner court of feelings which circumstances forever bar the historian from entering. So it is with individual conduct. In Goethe's *Wilhelm Meister* one of the characters, *Aurelia,* gives the highest possible praise to her uncle's intellectual powers, and then says: "With me he did not prosper quite so well, for here the question was about emotions, of which he had not a glimpse; and with whatever tolerance and sympathy and rationality he spoke about my sentiments, it was palpable to me that he had not the slightest notion of what formed the ground of all my conduct."

One of the greatest achievements of the new psychology is to reverse the conception that reason is fundamental in man. The second great advance is to be found in the vast recent developments in the study of the endocrine glands and their relation to emotional life. Their almost incomprehensible power, their multiple relations and variations give us a glimpse of the staggering complexity of the emotions. Now add to this the biological and instinctive affinities and antagonisms—all of which must operate in a complex environment where intellect has outrun the emotional life.

Complex feelings in literature confront us everywhere. Almost every example we have so far given reveals something of this complexity.

THE SORROWS OF WERTHER. Here is a little work [28] said to have been written in three weeks while Goethe was under an intense emotional strain. It contains almost every emotion known to psychology. What is more it contains them in their proper combinations, development, and strength. It is simply a series of letters written by Werther. The author claims only to have collected and presented them. The suicides it is said to have caused in Germany were due chiefly to outside misrepresentation and interpretation.

Nowhere could we find a more readable and clear presentation of the semi-blind urges that lie behind action than in this simple quotation:

"All learned professors and doctors are agreed that children do not comprehend the cause of their desires; but that the grown-up should wander about this earth like children, without knowing whence they come, or whither they go, influenced as little by fixed motives, but guided like them by biscuits, sugar-plums, and the rod,— this is what nobody is willing to acknowledge; and yet I think it is palpable."

"Yes, my dear Wilhelm, nothing on this earth affects my heart so much as children. When I look on at their doings; when I mark in the little creatures the seeds of all those virtues and qualities which they will one day find so indispensable; when I behold in the obstinate all the future firmness and constancy of a noble character; in the capricious, that levity and gayety of temper which will carry them lightly over the dangers and troubles of life, their whole nature simple and unpolluted,—then I call to mind the golden words of the Great Teacher of mankind, 'Unless ye become like one of these!' And now, my friend, these children, who are our equals, whom we ought to consider as our models, we treat them as though they were our subjects. They are allowed no will of their own. And have we, then, none ourselves? Whence comes our exclusive right? Is it because we are older and more experienced? Great God! from the height of thy heaven thou beholdest great children and little children, and no others; and thy Son has long since declared which afford thee greatest pleasure. But they believe in Him, and hear Him not,—that, too, is an old story; and they train their children after their own image, etc."

Every day we read in the papers of awful crimes, murders, and suicides. The populace criticize and judge *according to their own feelings.* Or rather, they assume that the criminal had the same feelings and emotions as they now have. They pronounce judgment in advance of the courts and judges. Their *feeling* of certainty leads them to assume that they know more about it than the judge and jury who hear the evidence. A decision of the Supreme Court is condemned by those who do not know the first line of the Constitution. Psychology has no task equal to the correction of this state of mind.

In this tragedy a modern up-to-date analysis of the freedom of the will is made. Albert, a cold, formalistic lawyer is arguing with Werther about suicide. Werther is arguing that human nature has its limits and that there are diseases of mind as real as of the body. He tells Albert that he does not understand how feelings and ideas work their destiny. That they too operate under law. Albert claimed that he was too general, then he draws this powerful concrete example which we all need to digest. He pictures a once happy and hopeful girl, but now abandoned by her lover :—

"All is darkness around her. No prospect, no hope, no consolation—forsaken by him in whom her existence was centered! She sees nothing of the wide world before her, thinks nothing of the many individuals who might supply the void in her heart; she feels herself deserted, forsaken by the world; and, blinded and impelled by the agony which wrings her soul, she plunges into the deep, to end her sufferings in the broad embrace of death.

"Shame upon him who can look on calmly, and exclaim, 'The foolish girl! she should have waited; she should have allowed time to wear off the impression; her despair would have been softened, and she would have found another lover to comfort her.' One might as well say, 'The fool, to die of a fever! why did he not wait till his strength was restored, till his blood became calm? all would then have gone well, and he would have been alive now.' " COMPLEXITY OF EMOTIONS IN *MAC-BETH*:—

We have already referred to Shakespeare as portraying the complexity of the emotions in their most delicate relations. The play opens with a combination of superstitious awe and the fear of nature—the Witches accompanied by a terrific storm.

> "When shall we three meet again
>   In thunder, lightning, or in rain?"

Macbeth's first words are:

> "So foul and fair a day I have not seen."

What a strange combination of emotions! But even some psychologists have suggested that there is in many cases a relation between distressing internal conditions and happy external conditions which hastens suicide. The supernatural idea stimulates the notion of guilt in Macbeth. Yet his envy, jealousy, and self-elation impulses overpower other feelings when the King announces that Malcolm will be his successor.

Act One opens with feelings of agitation and dread. Banquo says:

> "A heavy summons lies like lead upon me,
>   And yet I would not sleep. Merciful powers,
>   Restrain in me the cursed thoughts that nature
>   Gives way to in repose!"

Lady Macbeth's courage does not come from a shameless lack of the better impulses. It springs from her sense of duty to help her husband and from the imaginative influence of the future. But even this iron will is later on overwhelmed by remorse.

Does not all this bear a striking relation to many things happening around us every day? Various crimes are carefully planned and carried out. But nothing like the same order of intelligence accompanies the escape. Nietzsche expresses it best: "One thing is deed, another is the picture of the deed."

Think of the complex emotions on which Mark Antony plays to arouse the Romans. But it is not unlike what the skillful political orator does today. These examples indicate that great literary writers have handled the emotions well. Sometimes a natural insight unconsciously guides them, especially in stories. The keenest psychological analysis aims to dissect the human heart. Ibsen is always dissecting complex emotions.

In this connection it is interesting to see how deeply Euripides dived into the complex emotions. His tragedy —Medea [29] aims directly at the emotional life. This tragedy of human emotions finds a striking parallel in Schiller's early and fiery play, The Robbers. The very opening speech delivered by the Nurse plunges us into the tragic influence of strong emotions. She is lamenting the fate of Medea who claims to have saved the life of Jason on the ship Argo, to have married him in Greece. Later they were banished to the land of Corinth. Here Jason decides to marry the daughter of the King.

For pages the reader's sympathy is brought to the highest pitch for this unfortunate woman. Her sorrow seems to be so genuine. But, alas, another psychological side of her life is revealed. Her agony seems supreme when King Creon comes to tell her that she and her two children are banished from the land. By her witching arts she prevails on him to let her stay another day.

Hatred and jealousy now take full possession of her. She plans the death of the whole family. But now what city will receive her! She is an exile from Hellas, for in her own land she murdered her own brother. However, hate and jealousy are not amenable to reason.

Jason comes and tries to explain to her that he is not going to marry the princess for her sake nor for any selfish purpose, but to give them position, standing, and wealth as exiles in a foreign land. He tells her that not for anything she has said against him is she to be banished, but because she could not hold her tongue from slander of the rulers. He pleads with her to be silent, but if she will not he wishes her to take money for her exile. She will believe none of it, pronounces him a traitor and bids him depart.

About this time she suddenly hails Aegeus, a former friend who has long been married, but still childless. After each tells their story, she proposes to perform her fiendish work, return and marry him. She now sends for Jason, her husband, and with great deception tells him that she repents her conduct, that she wishes him well, will accept his aid, and that she intends to send some presents to the Princess by the two boys and have them plead with her to spare the children from banishment. Her deception works like a charm. Death is now on her brain, death to all but Jason.

The dominance of emotion over reason is one of the first psychological principles that confronts the modern student. The old psychology believed in the supremacy of the intellect except in undisciplined minds. Now the power of feeling over the whole mental life is one of the chief revelations of modern psychology. The feelings of hate, envy, jealousy, anger, and selfishness are the spurs to even the highest reaches of intellectual activity. In short even in genius, the intellect is found to operate under the guidance of many complex feelings.

COMPLEX AND CONFLICTING EMOTIONS. Emotional or intellectual activity is valuable in proportion to its relation to the vital problems of human life. The surest method of securing this active mental condition, as against the passive state of absorption, is an appeal to complex and conflicting emotions. We have here the complex emotions of pity, sorrow, despair, love, hate, jealousy, maternal affection, and vengeance. The reader is first wrought up with a powerful sympathy for a wronged and sorrow-ladened mother. But soon this apparently saintly and submissive soul seems to contain a perfect villain also. You even doubt if her sorrow is sincere. Fewer places in literature can you find a better example of what Ribot calls a successive contradictory character. She is swayed by conflicting emotions. This she well expresses when she is on the very eve of carrying out her crime:

> Women, my strength is gone,
> Gone like a dream, since I looked upon
> Those shining faces . . . I can do it not.
> What is it with me? Would I be a thing
> Mocked at, and leave mine enemies to sting
> Unsmitten? It must be. O coward heart,
> Even to harbor such soft words!

CHAPTER XI

SUBTLE PSYCHOLOGY AND SUGGESTION IN LITERATURE

FEW SUBJECTS ARE of more practical and public interest than the one we are about to consider. But would it be possible to find another subject concerning which there is such a diversity and confusion of opinion? Opinions range all the way from hard-headed skepticism about well-established facts to a faith that disregards law and common sense. It is a field in which people are inclined to believe either too much or too little. Some entirely deny the scientific facts of hypnotism and ignore the daily manifestations of suggestion. Others accept without question all the miraculous reports about hypnotism and mental healing.[30]

DEGREES OF SUGGESTIBILITY. Not only do different individuals differ in their susceptibility to suggestion, but the same individual varies under different conditions. There are many degrees of suggestibility, ranging from the lowest to the highest, which is found in thoroughly hypnotized subjects.

1. In ordinary waking life everyone is amenable to suggestion in some degree. The examples are legion, and may be verified a thousand times under the simplest conditions. Suggestibility is the power behind imitation, in both its conscious and its unconscious forms. Ideas and images may be unconsciously received and acted upon. The whole field of unconscious imitation belongs here. The best methods of training children rely for the most

part on well-directed suggestion. Character and conduct are largely results of suggestion.

Children are more amenable to direct suggestion than are adults, who have learned by experience when to be on their guard. But even adults are open to thousands of suggestions, especially if they come in indirect ways. Daily we declare that we have "made up our minds" to do so and so, when in reality the decision may have resulted from the shrewd suggestion of others, made "when the iron was hot."

2. All writers on social psychology now declare an increased suggestibility to exist in a crowd: the critical faculty is greatly weakened; the exciting cause absorbs all attention. Le Bon says, "The impossible does not exist for a crowd." This, he thinks, accounts for the creation and propagation of improbable legends and stories. Affirmation, repetition, and contagion are the needed factors in exciting the social organism.

3. We are indebted to Dr. Sidis for the third general form of suggestion. Suggestibility is intensified in the passive, semiwaking, or "subwaking" state. Dr. Sidis distinguishes this form of suggestion from hypnotism, and calls it "hypnoidization." Name it what we will, it exists and must be taken into account. The early idea that hypnotic suggestion has no effect while the subject is still conscious of his surroundings has been long since proven false. Several physicians who once used hypnotism now maintain that hypnotic sleep is unnecessary; they maintain that suggestion is equally effective for medical purposes before the sleep stage.

For practical purposes, then, we should differentiate by recognizing *waking suggestion, subwaking suggestion, crowd suggestion,* and *hypnotic suggestion.* Bernheim has abandoned the use of the term *hypnotism,* and recognizes instead degrees of suggestibility.

Let us glance at the use which literature has made of this universal fountain of human conduct. The biological urges and the complex emotional life which we have considered furnish the background for the direction and operation of suggestion. Especially do all forms of the instinct for self-preservation, such as fear, self-interest, and sex furnish a ready response to suggestion. Does not *Pippa Passes* illustrate a great principle of modern psychology—the power of unconscious suggestion? Early in the morning of New Year's Day poor Pippa is looking forward to her only holiday of the year; she hopes all will be well. This poor factory girl spends her day in the simple manner of going about singing the songs that lie deepest in her soul. Early in the morning Sebald and Ottima, whose end has just been accomplished by the murder of Ottima's husband, are suffering from a revulsion of feeling. Ottima, however, has just succeeded in diverting Sebald's mind when Pippa passes, singing "God's in his heaven." All unconsciously this operates on Sebald's stricken conscience and he kills himself; Ottima offers a prayer for him and does likewise.

Later Pippa passes Jules, who, by trick of his fellow students, has had a woman of inferior rank and blemished reputation imposed upon him as a wife. He has just found it out and is going to desert her. Pippa passes, singing. Jules suddenly decides to change his mind, to let revenge go, to love his wife and seek a new life in her own country. In the evening Luigi's mother is trying to persuade her son not to carry out his intention to assassinate the king. She has about succeeded when Pippa passes and sings a song which unconsciously fortifies his wavering purpose. The deed is done. Again, her song prevents Monsignor from carrying out his intention to murder the Intendant of the cathedral palace. Monsignor had allowed himself to be drawn into a plot with the

Intendant to rob Pippa of her inheritance. He was just about to permit Pippa to be enticed to Rome to a life of shame and, indirectly, death. Just before Pippa passes, the Intendant says, "Is it a bargain?"

The day is spent; she returns to her room at night, wondering if she could ever touch these people "magnificent in sin." She is all unconscious of the danger she has escaped from those lying in wait for her, or of the influence she has exerted. And those whose destinies have been sealed by her songs are all unaware of the real cause.

Literature continually shows us that life and conduct are under the power of a great network of forces both conscious and unconscious to us? Psychology is a study of human life; literature is life objectified and set to the music of other souls.

Here we have a form of subtle psychology with which daily life is filled. The formalistic psychologist either ignores it because it cannot be reduced to graphs, statistics and curves, or else he fails to comprehend it. How will any amount of graphs, curves, and tables help the average individual to understand corrupt politics? Will such psychology ever reveal the methods by which poor humanity has been brought to believe absurd religious dogmas, or how fear, self-interest, and supposed future good dominate our conduct in relation to each other? How will such psychology help us to understand that both the North and the South, although holding directly opposite views during the Civil War, could be honest and sincere? It is that kind of psychology that the average individual needs. Subtle psychology is what counts in conduct and the evolution of morals. Such psychology depends upon the great field of suggestion.

To divorce objective and introspective psychology is a disastrous blunder. To lift the masses out of the age-long false ideas about human conduct it is necessary to stimulate honest introspection. For the realization of this purpose literature is the best means yet devised, and in it *suggestion* is one of the chief arts employed.

THE RUBAIYAT, SUGGESTION AND SUBTLE PSYCHOLOGY. Sarcasm is a dangerous weapon, but in the hands of a genius its use has been a successful method of provoking thought. Molière and Voltaire used this weapon like a two-edged sword. But the most widely known form of it is the *Rubaiyat* of Omar Khayyam, the learned Persian astronomer. In literature some of the keenest suggestions are given by means of single words and phrases. As we have seen, the use of symbolism is entirely dependent upon the psychology of suggestion. However, it is often accumulative, striking first in one direction then in another at supposed superstitions or false beliefs. Omar sees law everywhere as opposed to chaotic freedom. His sarcasm is directed chiefly against the ancient ideas of Creation, Responsibility, and the Future.

> "Some for the Glories of This World; and some
> Sigh for the Prophet's Paradise to come;
> Ah, take the Cash, and let the Credit go,
> Nor heed the rumble of a distant drum!"

NIETZSCHE'S SUBTLE SARCASTIC SUGGESTIONS. Attention has already been paid to Nietzsche's powerful symbolism. Some of his suggestions and symbols are so obscure as to require a study of the whole discourse and even then they remain susceptible of many interpretations.[31]

STRINDBERG'S MASTERY OF SUGGESTION. Strindberg[32] is the most powerful, the most conscious and determined psychologist in all literature. He is in a class with Goethe, who said that he had felt himself capable of all the crimes of mankind. Besides this he was a careful student of evolution, biology, and medicine. He was by nature religious, yet he found no comfort in the dogmas of religion. In early life he loved women and endowed them with loyalty and devotion. But later he painted one of the most vicious women in all literature.

Max Stiner's extreme individualism stirred Strindberg's blood. His rebellion against Ibsen drove him by degrees to the naturalistic, realistic drama. This giant mind produced some fifty volumes that dive into the mysteries of body and mind, into historic and philosophic criticisms, and especially into the subtle psychology of suggestion, in the use of which he remains unsurpassed. In dozens of cases suggestion controls the destiny of his characters.

Notwithstanding our lengthy consideration of Strindberg there is one more example of keen subtle psychology that should be presented. *The Link* represents a divorce case and presents subtle psychology that is displayed in our court rooms hundreds of times every day. The Judge under whom the case is to be heard seeks out the Parson to get some idea of the case. The Pastor tells the Judge that when he heard one he believed one thing and when he heard the other he knew nothing about it. The Judge inquired if there would not be witnesses.

Pastor: No, they are not accusing each other in public. And furthermore: two false witnesses will furnish sufficient proof, and a perjurer will do just as well. Do you think I would base my judgment on servant gossip, on the loose-tongued chatter of envious neighbors, or on the spiteful partisanship of relatives?

Judge: You are a terrible sceptic, Pastor.

Pastor: Well, one gets to be so after sixty, and particularly after having tended souls for forty years. The habit of lying clings like original sin, and I believe that all men lie. As children we lie out of fear; as grown-ups, out of interest, need, instinct for self-preservation; and I have known those who lied out of sheer kindliness. In the present case, and so far as this married couple is concerned, I fear you will find it very hard to figure out who has told most of the truth, and all I can do is to warn you against being caught in the snares set by preconceived opinions. You were married not so long ago yourself, and you are still under the spell of the young woman's witchery. For this reason you may easily become prejudiced in favor of a young and charming lady, who is an unhappy wife and mother besides. On the other hand, you have recently become a father, and as such you cannot escape being moved by the impending separation of the father from his child. Beware of sympathy with either side, for sympathy with one is cruelty to the other.

The Father is one of the most powerful tragedies ever written. The play pictures the situation of a Captain, his wife Laura and their only child Bertha, the Nurse and servants. His wife is determined to rule or ruin. She lets nothing stand in the way of achieving her purpose. The very opening of the play gives the keynote of the suggestion that is to rule throughout. It is one of the finest examples of a suggestion taking unconscious hold of a mind and appearing later in another form.

One of the servants under the Captain has committed a moral offense for which the Captain reprimands him. The servant hints that others may be to blame. The Captain asked him definitely if he is not the father of the child. He then adroitly raises the question if any man knows that he is the father of any particular child. The Captain sees that Bertha, his daughter, is living a miserable life dominated by Laura's mother who tries to make the child act the part of a spiritualistic medium. She keeps Bertha up until late morning hours. He determines to send her away and Laura is equally determined that she shall not go. His wife sends for the Doctor and begins at once to *suggest* to the Doctor that the Captain is mentally ill. She tells the doctor that they have been married twenty years and that he has never once made a decision without changing his mind afterward.

Laura: Can't I? Do you really think I would trust my daughter to wicked people to have her taught that every thing her mother implanted in her child is mere foolishness? Why, afterwards, she would despise me all the rest of her life!

Captain: Do you think that a father should allow ignorant and conceited women to teach his daughter that he is a charlatan?

Laura: It means less to the father. Because the mother is closer to the child, as it has been discovered that no one can tell for a certainty who the father of a child is.

Captain: How does that apply to this case?

Laura: You do not know whether you are Bertha's father or not.

Captain: I do not know?

Laura: No; what no one knows, surely you cannot know.

Captain: Are you joking?

Laura: No; I am only making use of your own teaching. For that matter, how do you know that I have not been unfaithful to you.

Laura tells the doctor that her husband has developed the fixed idea that he is not Bertha's father. When questioned by the Doctor, the Captain says:

"Didn't you feel ridiculous as a father? I know of

nothing so ludicrous as to see a father leading his children by the hand around the streets, or to hear a father talk about his children. 'My wife's children' he ought to say. Did you ever feel how false your position was? Weren't you ever afflicted with doubts, I won't say suspicious, for, as a gentleman, I assume that your wife was above suspicion."

When Laura sees the awful end to which all is destined she tries to untie the psychological knot but in vain. She says: "And as for your suspicions about the child they are absolutely false—" But nothing can prevent the awful climax tragedy.

I do not believe that any flaw can be found in this psychology of suggestion. It is true to all the modern knowledge we have of suggestion. Sadly enough, it is only too true to life and is duplicated thousands of times in some degree. Furthermore I do not believe that any psychologists can teach suggestion in a more forcible form.

HAMLET'S SUBTLE PLAY. Nowhere in literature do we have a more subtle and well-planned effort to produce definite results by suggestion than in *Hamlet* when Shakespeare has Hamlet put on a play to trap the King and Queen. The whole scheme as well as the play itself is saturated with suggestion.

The climax of suggestion is reached in that psychological play devised by Hamlet for the King and Queen.

Hamlet: Madam, how like you this play?
Queen: The lady protests too much, methinks.
Hamlet: O, but she'll keep her word.
King: Have you heard the argument? Is there no offence in't?
Hamlet: No, no, they do but jest, poison in jest. No offence i' the world.

King: What do you call the play?
Hamlet: The Mouse-trap. Marry, how? Tropically. This
          play is the image of a murder done in Vienna.
          Gonzago is the duke's name; his wife, Baptista.
          you shall see anon. 'Tis a knavish piece of work,
          but what o' that? Your majesty and we that
          have free souls, it touches us not. Let the gall'd
          jade wince, our withers are wrung.

We might extend this investigation of suggestion in
literature indefinitely. Of course many writers use it to
very poor effect. This is clearly demonstrated in a book
by Collins, called *The Doctor Looks into Literature*. He
considers that these writers will never be classified as
literary geniuses or as real students of human conduct.

All that we have presented in former chapters illustrates the wise use of subtle suggestion. Symbolism is
only a form of suggestion. Deep emotional life is the
ever present background of suggestion. Thousands of
cases of insanity originate in suggestion built on a deep
emotional life. Suggestion explains the success of the
medicine-man and the miracles of mental healing. Some
day we will have a master work on *Religious Beliefs as a
Result of Suggestion*. We also have the extensive claims
of Freudian psychology that success in various forms
originates from suggestion in early life. The good or bad
effect of literature upon us is largely determined by its
suggestibility.

MARCEL PROUST AS PSYCHOLOGIST: Here is
a writer so absorbed by the psychological approach that
it is hard to label his works. Analytical psychology per-
vades all of them. He was born about the same time as
modern psychology—1871. His father was a physician.
He was related to the philosopher Bergson, and this
influence is evident. His characters are not finished prod-

ucts: they are ever in the process of creation. His greatest work is *Remembrance of the Past*. Out of this he elaborated a psychological novel that grew to eleven volumes. He seems to have believed in something akin to Herring's biological memory. His method has been designated as "accidental recovery of sensations which signify the core of our personality locked in the body." It is a form of intuitive psychology. In his portrayal of society he is similar to Balzac.

His psychology is to a certain extent like that of Samuel Butler and of Maeterlinck—somewhat mystical. But so long as there is interest in psychology there will be interest in Proust. He took the apparent chaos of his past memories and wove them into a great literary composition. He seems to follow William James, who declared that we never really forget anything.

In Butler's *The Way of All Flesh* we read: "I fancy that there is some truth in the view that is being put forward nowadays that it is our less conscious thoughts and our less conscious actions which mainly mould our actions."

Some one has said that a work of art has value in proportion to the experiences it awakens in us. If this be the standard of criticism then *Remembrance of the Past* will always have its place in world literature.

CHAPTER XII

FREE WILL AND LITERATURE

HERE CURRENT PSYCHOLOGY and the best of literature part company more noticeably than in any other field. Owing to the long standing belief that free will is necessary for a sense of responsibility, and to the same popular religious idea, psychology has for the most part either ignored or dodged this important problem. As a pioneer psychologist, James presented volumes that deny the freedom of the will as presented in religious theology, but later he concluded that although we cannot prove freedom, we should assert it for its moral value. That is almost equivalent to saying that science is working against the good of humanity. Professor More does much the same thing: after presenting most convincing facts from physiological and abnormal psychology, he feels compelled to offer a concluding chapter on freedom of the will. It is only an effort to make a medieval dogma respectable by throwing over it a scientific cloak. The same thing has been done by Collins and Babbitt in their attempt to introduce into literary criticism what they call *The New Humanism*.[33]

Their assumptions are: an inherent sense of decorum, free will, purpose, and rational guidance of conduct. However, it is perfectly clear that they were driven to assume this foundation. To assume, as P. E. More finally does, that religious authority is the basis of the

New Humanism is to carry us back to medieval think-ing. To assume that the Greeks were by some strange gift of the gods blessed with an intuition of true decorum, is not much better. Aristotle was perhaps one of the greatest scholar that ever walked the earth. However, he was no more than human. To believe that the great minds of art, music, literature and morals have long since passed away is too pessimistic for growing souls. The Middle Ages furnish us with an example of a whole civilization overcome by an inferiority complex.

When Mr. Babbitt says that free will "must simply be accepted as a mystery that may be studied in its practical effect," he has stepped upon dangerous ground. Psychologists have invited all theorists to join them in a search for "its practical effects." The psychologist says, "Show me a simple act where adequate causes for its performance cannot be found in man's natural instincts, in his training, in his surroundings, in his physical and emotional make-up, in the sum total of his mental rela-tions, in the unconscious driving force of his endocrine glands." The world famed physician Lorand declared that "Will power always means healthy thyroid, adrenal, and sexual glands." This statement made twenty-five or thirty years ago would undoubtedly be supplemented today by many factors—all of which reenforce it.

Biological responsibility has been ignored by theology, and not even suspected by the populace. Do not animals assume a responsibility for the protection and feeding of their young? Responsibility is an evolutionary product to the end of securing certain lines of conduct. It is a force just as much under law as any other force. In our modern complex society responsibility becomes largely a matter of conforming to artificial laws made to regulate conduct. But the length to which responsibility goes depends entirely upon the biological and traditional forces in human nature. *This is the inevitable foundation of all tragedy.*

Real literature does not exist without the assumption that mind, emotions and instincts are under law. Indeed the whole science of psychology is impossible if this is not true: even the assumption of a limited field of true freedom of the will, without those limits being defined, makes uncertain any conclusions of psychology.

All literature is founded on the assumption of the relation between internal forces and external conditions. As we have already seen, Greek literature is dominated by the idea of fate. But fate is only another word for the internal forces of instinct and physiological conditions. No matter how these internal forces may be conceived they exist under certain laws of development and manifestation. Modern biology and psychology have much to say about will, but not free will. Will is the result of all the forces operating on an organism at any one time.

All real literature is true. That is to say, given the external and internal conditions as portrayed the destiny is inevitable. Othello, Hamlet, Macbeth march to their inevitable destiny under the power of their heredity, their past experiences, and the conditions in which they are placed.

I have already called attention to the fact that some writers make the internal forces dominant. As a rule the Greeks determined destiny almost independently of outer conditions. But that was only their dim surmise of the biological and hereditary background. Shakespeare mixes the ideas of fate and heredity, but the introduction of fate is largely a concession to popular psychology. While Ibsen recognized the force of internal conditions he endeavored to picture will as overcoming environment. These writers probably believed that they were defending freedom, but they overlooked the fact that the internal life may be determined just as much as the external conditions.

On the other hand writers like Hugo, Tolstoy, Dostoievsky, and Galsworthy have exalted the influence of the environment. These two extremes accord with modern psychology. Psychologists recognize that all organisms are exactly what heredity and environment have made them. Yet there is great divergence of opinion as to the relative influence of these forces. The faction emphasizing environment overlooks the fact that this very environment has been developed and established in accord with the deep instincts and impulses of the race, that adjustment is mainly fitting into some modified form of original nature. They also forget that even the weaklings who are readily swallowed up by the environment owe their weakness as a general rule to heredity.

If any one doubts literary insight into psychology and the laws of human conduct let him read the plays of the three great dramatists of the Greeks—Sophocles, Euripides, and Aeschylos. The entire Hellenic world honored Sophocles until his plays reached the civilized nations of three continents. He studied human nature more profoundly than any one of his time. He saw clearly the conflict between nature and man—or what we now call heredity and environment. With a calm serenity, like that of Marcus Aurelius, he took "a glance into the secret and terrible things of nature." In all these tragedies there is the suggestion that reason should be supreme. But there would still exist accident, misery, and death. However, purpose backed by feeling gives reason force. This is modern psychology.

> *Creon.* What chance is this, with which my coming fits?
> *Guard.* Men, O my king, should pledge themselves to
>   nought;

For cool reflection makes their purpose void.
I surely thought I should be slow to come here,
Cowed by threats, which then fell thick on me;
But now persuaded by the sweet delight
Which comes unlooked for, and beyond our hopes,
I come, although I swore the contrary.

When *Antigone* is brought before her accusers she digs deeper into the inexorable laws of nature.

Antig. I own I did it, and will not deny.
Creon. (To guard) Go thou thy way, where'er thy will
    may choose,
    Freed from a weighty charge. (Exit guard)
      (To Antigone)
    And now for thee.
    Say in a few words, not lengthening out thy speech,
    Knew'st thou the edicts which forbade these things?
Antig. I knew them. Could I fail? Full clear were they.
Creon. And thou did'st dare to disobey these laws?
Antig. Yes, for it was not Zeus who gave them forth,
    Nor Justice, dwelling with the Gods below,
    Who traced these laws for all the sons of men;
    Nor did I deem thy edicts strong enough,
    That thou, a mortal man, should'st ever-pass
    The unwritten laws of God that know not change.
Messenger. Ye men of Cadmos and Amphion's house,
    I know no life of mortal man which I
    Would either praise or blame. 'Tis Fortune's chance
    That raiseth up, and Fortune bringeth low,
    The man who lives in good or evil plight;
    And prophet of men's future there is none.

Euripides dived into the modern psychological problems of sex and instinct. He understood the dangers of sex

repression. In the tragedy *Electra* he is realistic, socialistic and altogether modern. The inevitable play of selfishness, desire for vengeance, and sex weave a network of
determining forces.

Aeschylos busied himself with problems of heredity,
evil, guilt, and the laws of nature. In *Prometheus Bound*
are these lines:

Chor. Who guides the helm, then, of Necessity?
Prom. Fates triple-formed, Errinyes unforgetting.
Chor. Is Zeus, then, weaker in his might than these?
Prom. Not even He can 'scape the thing decreed.
Chor. What is decreed for Zeus but still to reign?
Prom. Thou may'st no further learn, ask thou no more.
Chor. 'Tis doubtless some dread secret which thou hidest.
Prom. Of other theme make mention, for the time
      Is not yet come to utter this, but still
      It must be hidden to the uttermost;
      For by thus keeping it it is that I
      Escape my bondage foul, and these my pains.

The tragedies of these three great writers are dominated by a psychological insight that will make them live
forever. When we note that these writers lived and
wrote before they had any chance to profit by the philosophical and scientific works of Socrates, Plato, and
Aristotle their genius and natural insight into human
nature becomes more evident.

Goethe's *Faust* furnishes one of the finest examples in
literature, of determinism resulting from a balancing of
the internal and external forces. Faust's turbulent internal
nature reaches a happy equilibrium in the second part by
the play of all the forces of nature and of society.

There is another aspect of this great network of forces

determining human conduct. The percentage of human destinies determined by this almost universally neglected condition of existence is undoubtedly very large. I refer to the chance happenings of life. This does not mean chance in the sense of having no cause—such a thing does not exist—but rather chance in the sense that no one foresaw or planned the event. Millions of deaths, successes, crimes, joys and sorrows result from such chance happenings. They in turn set up other lines of events.

Many such cases are woven unconsciously into literature, and several writers have made a special effort to give them prominence. Conrad presents the problem in *Chance*. Mark Twain drives the lesson home with a vengeance in his *Mysterious Stranger*.[34] Three boy playmates have been joined by another who turns out to be Satan. Along toward the close of the work Satan surprises two of the boys by telling them that Nikolaus would die in twelve days. They begged of Satan to know why. He told them that it was best for he could see what a dreadful life he would live. Satan closed their mouths so they could not say a word about it. But they knew it was bound to occur.

But how could it happen! He was young, well and happy—even was planning a party on the day that was to be his funeral. The boys went every day and spent all day playing until late in the evening.

The evening of the last appointed day they all stay out late. The father whips Nikolaus and tells him that he cannot go out for three days. The next day the boys come to play with him until the appointed hour. The clock is about ready to strike ten, when the mother opens the door and calls to Nickolaus that the neighbor's girl has fallen into the river and that he should run down and help her out. They are both drowned in the river.

James Cabell in his *Beyond Life* provides an escape from the self-deception based on chance under what he calls the Demiurge to Romance.[35]

"Indeed, when I consider the race to which I have the honor to belong, I am filled with respectful wonder. . . . All about us flows and gyrates unceasingly the material universe,—an endless inconceivable jumble of rotatory blazing gas and frozen spheres and detonating comets, where through spins Earth like a frail midge. And to this blown molecule adhere what millions and millions and millions of parasites just such as I am, begetting and dreaming and slaying and abnegating and toiling and making mirth, just as did aforetime those countless generations of our forebears, every one of whom was likewise a creature just such as I am!"

Then at the very close of the book he says:

"We are being made into something quite unpredictable, I imagine: and through the purging and the smelting, we are sustained by an instinctive knowledge that we are being made into something better. For this we know, quite incommunicably, and yet as surely as we know that we will to have it thus.

"And it is this will that stirs in us to have the creatures of earth and the affairs of earth, not as they are, but 'as they ought to be,' which we call romance. But when we note how visibly it sways all life we perceive that we are talking about God."

THE MODERN SOCIAL DRAMA. The modern social drama has brought the problem of human freedom to the front. The literary treatment of social conduct and crime either leans to environment as the chief determining factor, puts the main emphasis on heredity, or sees the outcome as a balancing of the inner biological forces with the outer conditions. The last explanation is the only defensible interpretation of human conduct.

Literature has done more to hasten a modification of our barbaric penal codes than any other one thing. Galsworthy's *Justice* compelled a modification of the English treatment of criminals. Hugo threw the chief emphasis on environment and went so far as to say that society has just such criminals as she provides for.

LONELY LIVES BY HAUPTMANN. Here was a writer most human and universal. He shows how individual differences, early training, complexity of modern beliefs—unconsciously set a whole family of five, all of whom mean well, against each other.

DOES THE DRAMA REPRESENT DAILY LIFE? It may be argued that when we go to the theatre and see seduction, assassination, suicide, murder—it is not life as we see it every day. Herein lies the real deterministic current of literature. Our private feelings and opinions live under the deep sea. It is the literary diver who reveals the real springs of human conduct. He shows us the hidden springs of conduct, the power of group emotions, how and why these groups vary, and their permanency throughout time.

Those who dive beneath the surface of life show us that evil comes not out of individual men and villains, but runs through men's souls. What we see on the stage is the accumulated tragedy of orderly underlying forces. While the surface may give the impression of actual confusion, disorder, and chaos the deep forces are an orderly on-going.

Individual destiny counts but little. The stream of life moves on. Life is a mixture of comedy and tragedy: some one has defined comedy as life seen at a distance and tragedy as life seen near at hand. Modern drama tends to mix the two. The pleasures, the joys, happy relations as well as the heartaches, the sorrows, sufferings, are one and all caused not by good or evil intentions, but as a result of conditions over which no single person has control.

The Russian writer Chekhov [36] dived into these problems to an extent not yet appreciated by American critics. He has no heroes and no villains—he presents life. He is an optimist even though his optimism lies ahead—as he often says, "in 300 years or more."

He says: "Day and night I am obsessed by the same persistent thought; I must write, I must write, I must write. . . . No sooner have I finished one story than I am somehow compelled to write another, then a third, after the third a fourth. I write without stopping, except to change horses like a postchaise. I have no choice. What is there brilliant or delightful in that. I should like to know? It's a dog's life! Here I am talking to you, excited and delighted, yet never for one moment do I forget that there is an unfinished story waiting for me indoors."

Eugene O'Neill reaches down into the submerged forces that determine human conduct in *Anna Christie*. *Chris* is captain of a small *barge*. All the time he is dreading the sea which he comes to call the *ole devil sea*. Yet under no condition does he give up sea life. He placed his only child with relations on a ranch near St. Paul, when she was very small. After twenty years or more he is in a low-down saloon in New York. Here he gets some mail and a letter from *Anna*. She is coming there to see him.

As she grew to maturity she was seduced by her cousin Paul. She spent two years in a house of ill-fame, but wrote her father that she was a nurse. When they met neither of them showed the feelings for each other that would seem natural. She told *Chris* that she had been sick. He insisted on taking her on the dirty *barge* with him—only men on board. He dreaded the sea both for himself and *Anna;* yet could not stay away from his barge.

Anna told him nothing. But she charged him with wanting to get rid of her. Finally the Irish stoker on board—*Mat Burke*—falls in love with *Anna. Mat* wants to marry her and *Chris* is enraged and wants to kill him. They come into port and *Mat* tells *Anna* that they are going to be married before the sun goes down. *Anna* tells him that she said good-bye when he first kissed her; that it cannot be—never.

Then she makes the two men sit down and tells them her sad story of betrayal and the life she has lived and that now she is going "to beat it." She tells them that she knows what they are thinking. Then she says: "And who's to blame for it, me or you? If you'd even acted like a man—if you'd even been a regular father and had me with you—maybe things would be different!" "But I got to thinking of you—and I couldn't take the train. So I came back—to wait some more. Can't you forgive what is dead and gone—and forget it?"

Finally *Mat* makes her swear that she never loved any of these men. Later he says:

"And I'm thinking 'twasn't your fault, maybe, but having that old ape for a father that left you to grow up alone, made you what you was. And if I could be believing 'tis only me you—"

Anna: "You got to believe it Mat. What can I do? I'll do anything."

It finally develops that both men have signed up to sail on the same boat. Mat and Anna are married and she tells them that she will make a home for them to come to.

His *Anna Christie* is an especially good illustration. The drama is said to be only life enlarged and reproduced in sequences. If this be true then the determining forces of life are inevitable.

CHAPTER XIII

PSYCHOLOGY OF CRIME IN LITERATURE

ALL LITERATURE HAS dealt with crime, but much of modern literature has turned specifically to the psychology of crime. Modern literature has been helpful in bringing about two important modifications of the popular mind— broadening of religious views and a new attitude towards crime.

What is the relation of criminal conduct to conduct in general? What is the relative part played by heredity and environment? Is there such a thing as *willful crime* in the sense that the individual had within him at the time something that might have prevented it without some internal or external change in conditions, in short, free-will? Do purely physical conditions such as endocrine conditions account for crime?

If heredity and environment are the sole factors in conduct why hold a man responsible or punish him? What leads to juvenile delinquency and how should it be treated? To what extent does the old idea of vengeance operate under the guise of individual reform or protection of society? Can we reform the criminal, and what kind of medicine is best adapted to that purpose? To what extent does the punishment of one criminal deter another? Does the publicity given to trials and punishments help to prevent crime or to hasten it? What part does suggesion play? Is crime really on the increase?

What kind of education will help most to prevent crime?

Before examining what literature has to say to these questions, let us state the probable answers. Our attitude towards the dependent and unfortunate has been one of growing concern and sympathy. No other country in the world has made such an effort to help these classes as have we. The prevention of crime and the proper punishment of the criminal are problems of deepest concern to society. Crime is only a part of conduct in general and scientific study is slowly creating a new attitude towards the criminal. But literature has done most of all to bring about this attitude.

NEW VIEW OF CRIME AND CRIMINALS:— Franklin K. Lane, Secretary of the Interior under President Wilson, said of the American prisons:

I have long thought that we dealt with criminals in a manner which tended to keep them as criminals and altogether opposed to the interests of society. I am not sentimental on this proposition, but I think I am sensible. We are dealing with men convicted of crime more harshly and more unreasonably than we deal with dogs. Our fundamental mistake is that we utterly ignore the fact that there is such a thing as psychology. We are treating prisoners with the methods of five hundred years ago, before anything was known about the nature of the human mind. . . . There are, of course, certain kinds of men who should, for society's sake, be kept in prison as long as they live, just as there are kinds of insane people that should be kept in insane asylums until they die. . . . Gradually a great change is coming over educated people. People once thought that crime was due entirely to deliberate intent. Even the insane were once considered to be willfully set in their ways. Innocent children were abused and beaten. No one knew or cared anything about their inherited weaknesses.

The new view of conduct began with discoveries about human nature. It was found that children, like animals, come into the world with natural tendencies that at first largely direct their activities. Tendencies to fear, to be angry, to fight, to possess, to surpass others, to hate— all furnish a background for later action. Many observers of human nature have called attention to the power of imitation and of habit. These natural tendencies are not bad in themselves: They are the only possible basis on which education and society can be built. But proper guidance is needed to insure the good of society.

There are natural tendencies that fit into and serve the community, and it is on these that we build our habits and education in order to check the tendencies that might become detrimental. Human beings have a natural tendency to be social, to sympathize with others, to wish the approval of others, to love home and country, to indulge in healthy and beneficial play, and to cooperate. It is these tendencies we must strengthen to prevent stealing, lying, hate, and violence. This new idea of human conduct is making us see the defective criminal in the same light as that in which the physician sees the sick and helpless.

PROTECTION OF SOCIETY. However, society must be protected, and it may be necessary to isolate the individual from society in order to provide that protection. Certainly the fact that punishment is severe does not prevent crime as we once thought it did. The swiftness and certainty of the punishment is much more important than the severity of the sentence

Mere punishment of crime does not protect law-abiding citizens. Neither does a spiteful attitude protect society. Such treatment makes the criminal worse and has a bad effect on those who prosecute him. Perhaps there are thousands of habitual criminals who should be permanently isolated from society even though their offenses are not serious. We protect society from other mentally disordered persons, the insane: why not from these?

Prison reform is not, as most people suppose, due to foolish sympathy for the criminal. It is, on the contrary, the only way to protect society from the vengeance of the criminal when he is freed. Thomas Mott Osbourne believes that 90 per cent of all prisoners go out determined to get even with society, chiefly on account of the treatment they receive in prison. We do not convince them that their punishment is an act of justice, nor do we create any dread of a possible return to prison.

THE HISTORIC ATTITUDE. It would be too horrifying to relate in detail all the history of the cruel treatment of the wrongdoer by society. The whole truth is by no means expressed in the statement: "An eye for an eye, and a tooth for a tooth." Revenge in ancient times had no such bounds. Whole families or tribes were often killed to avenge a single death. Medieval punishments are among the most horrible recorded in history. Various fines were imposed to pay the state and the person wronged, and a second and third fine imposed for non-payment of the first fine. When a man could not pay the fines he was sold as a slave, banished, or even put to death.

The jail is the oldest form of prison. Robinson, in his book "Penology in the United States," says the jail originated during the reign of Henry II. The jail is the place of confinement for all prisoners before sentence. Those convicted of serious crimes and sentenced for long periods are transferred to prison. It was only in about the year 1300 that prisons began to be constructed. The inmates were left in rags and filth, bound in chains, and placed in dungeons. Since this seemed to have no effect, more severe punishment was invented: limbs were broken and mutilated; public flogging became common. According to Robinson, Delaware still has 26 offenses for which flogging can be administered. At one time England had an incredible number of offenses for which the death penalty was inflicted. Under Henry VIII it is said that 263 crimes were punishable by death.

Now let us examine a few types of literature concerning these problems. If we are to accept our biblical literary record our first introduction to the human race has to do with crime. It is the violation of a prohibition that blocks one of the deepest instincts of human life. Almost the next is another crime resulting from the instincts of greed and gain, from jealousy, and from hate. It is murder, the beginning of war. From that day to this prohibitions have multiplied and brought about multiplication of crime. The Old Testament abounds in accounts of these prohibitions and their violations.

Hammurabi's Laws which ante-date the Laws of Moses by several hundred years contain nearly 100 prohibitions and penalties. "If a man carry on highway robbery and be captured he shall be put to death." "If a physician open an abscess near the eye and destroy the eye, one shall cut off his hands." "If a builder build a house for any one and does not build it solid; and the house which he has built, falls down and kills the owner: one shall put the builder to death."

Through the influence of Christ, the New Testament assumes a modern attitude towards crime. Without argument, without biological fact, Christ manifested the modern spirit toward the criminal. The climax was reached on the Cross when he said: "Father forgive them, for they know not what they do." He saw clearly that according to their traditions they could do nothing else. He intuitively understood human nature. His deepest psychological utterance is: "Judge not lest ye be judged."

But unthinking readers pass it over without suspecting its significance. Most of the disciples exhibited the same kind of insight, but by no means the same clearness and force.

Crime Among the Hindus. The life through which the Hindus passed prior to our historic records can only be conjectured. But we may guess that it was not dissimiliar to that of other peoples. When we first hear of them they are in a high state of civilization, and this was thousands of years before Christ.

Their literature is a great contrast to that of other early civilizations. One is struck by the comparative absence of crimes as seen in other literature. For high moral standards their literature is far above that of the *Iliad* or of Shakespeare.

It appears that sacredness of pledges or promises stood first in their ethical code. The sad banishment of Rama and finally of the saintly Sita is the result of a choice between violating an unwise and treacherous pledge and these woeful banishments.

In the Mahabharata there is only one outstanding wrongdoer—Sisupala.

Tiger-hearted Sisupala spake in anger stern and high,
Calm unto him Krishna answered, but a light was in his
    eye:

"List, O chiefs and righteous monarchs! from a daugh-
    ter of our race
Evil-destined Sisupala doth his noble lineage trace,

Spite of wrong and frequent outrage, spite of insult
    often flung,
Never in his heart hath Krishna sought to do his kins-
    man wrong.

Then the bright and whirling discus, as the mandate
    Krishna said,
Fell on impious Sisupala, from his body smote his
    head."

The internal causes working out their destiny give a
semblance of freedom. But from whatsoever source these
internal forces come they are an orderly accumulation,
and they manifest themselves according to law and order.
Almost every punishment is saturated with hate and the
spirit of vengeance. The idea of preventing other similar
crimes is present, but often it is only an excuse for hate
and vengence.

In *The Merchant of Venice* both sides are under the
spell of desire for vengeance. Race hatred runs high.

Shylock: "How like a fawning publican he looks.
    I hate him for he is a Christian;
    But more, for that in low simplicity
    He lends out money gratis, and brings down
    The rate of usance here with us in Venice.
    If I can catch him once upon the hip,
    I will feed fat the ancient grudge I bear him.
    He hates our sacred nations, and he rails,
    Even there where merchants most do congregate."
The Duke then appeals to Shylock's possible mercy:
Duke: "Make room, and let him stand before our face—
    Shylock, the world thinks, and I think so too,
    That thou but lead'st this fashion of thy malice
    To the last hour of act; and then 'tis thought
    Thou'lt show thy mercy and remorse, more strange
    Than is thy strange apparent cruelty."

We have said that Shakespeare has his characters act
according to their nature. It may be asked, "How then

do some of the characters in *King Lear*, in *Much Ado About Nothing*, in *Measure for Measure*, and in *All's Well that Ends Well*, act apparently so unpsychologically?" Some of them behave in what appear to be irrational ways. Some writers have found in the accepted ideas of the time adequate excuse for this variation. But even from the standpoint of modern psychology, is any justification necessary? Psychology has revealed marked individual differences. Long ago James called attention to the different will-types—the vacillating, the explosive, etc. Inconsistency and contradiction, at least on the surface, seem not uncommon in daily life. Daily the apparent contradictions of life baffle our imagination. That is why crime is so poorly understood today. We stand off and look at crime from our own supposedly rational standards.

It is doubtful whether Shakespeare wrote anything intentionally to present or teach any special doctrine. However, he does strongly suggest the modern psychological attitude towards the criminal and his treatment. That attitude is one of mercy and forgiveness on account of common human frailties.

Tolstoy constantly shows the bad psychological effect of punishment on those who punish as well as on those who are punished—the inhuman and hardening effect. This is made the central theme of his *Resurrection*. He pointed to the fact that most of us would be in jail if we got stern objective justice. *The Merchant of Venice* puts it equally strong—"that, in the course of justice, none of us should see salvation." Human frailties are so great, laws are so numerous and society is so complex that few can escape.

Tolstoy also shows the opposite in all his stories, the good effect on one who shows an understanding tolerance as well as on the one who receives such consideration.

This is especially evident today in the sympathetic treatment of juvenile delinquency. Judge Lindsey is the father of this psychological consideration of boys and girls in this country. Dozens of times have I seen him send boys to the reform school, accepting their word of honor to deliver themselves to the authorities miles away. Not long ago I heard a judge say that for eighteen years he sent men and women to prison with an attitude towards them which has since made him feel ashamed of himself. This proper human attitude is well presented in *The Merchant of Venice*.

But the most definite and far-reaching suggestions touching our modern psychology of crime Shakespeare presents in *Measure for Measure*—namely, crime as a result of human frailties. No criminal is so black as not to deserve human consideration. In the end Angelo, the arch criminal who confesses and pleads for death, is pardoned. It turns out that Claudio has not been put to death, as he thought, and both the women whom Angelo has wronged plead for his life. Even Barnadine "unfit to live or die" is granted mercy.

> "But for those earthly faults, I quit them all;
>   And pray thee take this mercy to provide
>   For better times to come."

The power of instinct to overcome ethical standards and to lead to what seems to be weakness is well expressed by Racine in his *Phèdre*.

As already stated the psychology of crime in modern literature is specific and definite. Outside of Tolstoy, who saw crime and misery as mainly due to tradition, superstition, and adverse environment, most Russian writers lay emphasis on biological heredity. Hugo, Galsworthy, Hauptmann, and others stress the environment as fundamental. Hugo's *Les Miserables* is famous for its minute analysis of the psychological forces in society.

Ibsen and Strindberg seem to recognize the two forces of heredity and environment. In *Ghosts* Ibsen uses both, but leaves the suggestion that crime is hereditary—even that acquired characteristics can be inherited, which modern biology denies. In *Hedda Gabler* we have a woman pushed on by impulses and instincts which she herself does not understand. She is an enigma to herself as well as to others. We have already seen how well Strindberg balances these two forces; in *Lonely Lives* the incidental forces for which no one is responsible are developed. All are agreed that some combination of these forces produces the criminal and the violations of our network of prohibitions.

There is universal agreement among psychologists that we should abandon the idea of punishment from the standpoint of abstract justice, vengeance or retribution. There will be no substantial reforms nor protection of society until the general public is brought to a realization of these facts. We are moving, but we are a long way off—perhaps two or three hundred years. We owe more to these writers than to any other class for the liberalized thinking which has been developed through their instigation.

Old religious dogmas stand as much in the way as any thing else. Psychology should recognize and welcome the great efforts of literature to bring about a new and better understanding of human nature and human conduct.

Psychologists in presenting their findings, often cease to be psychological. Why do we take so coolly the fact that 60,000 people are annually killed by automobiles? And why at the same time do we become so excited over the announcement that an unknown woman and her child went over an embankment sixty feet high and were burned to death under the car; that helpless people looked on while the shrieks of the dying could be heard blocks away? It is the individual picture, the living internal image, that excites response in us. To those who never heard or saw a radio a thousand statements of fact would not leave the impression that one personal contact does. Psychologists who attempt to appeal to individuals outside their own group would do well to point to at least one outstanding case or event on which attention could be centered and a feeling of warmth developed.

While Galsworthy's *Justice* throws emphasis on environment as the dominating cause of conduct, it is not wanting in suggestions concerning the part played by hereditary weaknesses and instincts. But the more far-reaching contention of the play has to do with temporary insanity cases. Psychology has long since learned that sane and insane are merely two flexible adjectives, capable of almost any extension or limitation—purely relative and only serving for a loose classification.

The whole of *Justice* is a careful psychological analysis of these forces. Falder is a well behaved honest young man in the employ of James How. He falls in love with Honeywill who is married to a man who beats and abuses her. But the English law will not allow her to get a divorce. They plan to run away and get married. He is in distress for money. He goes to the bank with a check for nine pounds, which he changes into ninety. He is arrested and brought to trial.

During the trial his defense attorney says: "If it please your lordship and gentleman of the jury, I am not going to dispute the fact that the prisoner altered this cheque, but I am going to put before you evidence as to the condition of his mind, and to submit that you would not be justified in finding that he was responsible for his actions at the time. I am going to show you, in fact, that he did this in a moment of aberration, amounting to temporary insanity, caused by violent distress under which he was labouring. Gentlemen, the prisoner is only twenty-three years old, I shall call before you a woman from whom you will learn the events that led up to this act. You will hear from her own lips the tragic infatuation with which she has inspired the prisoner. This woman, gentlemen, has been leading a miserable existence with a husband who habitually ill-uses her, from whom she actually goes in terror of her life. I am not, of course, saying that it's right or desirable for a young man to fall in love with a married woman, or that it's his business to rescue her from an ogre-like husband. I'm not saying anything of the sort. But we all know the power of the passion of love; and I would ask you to remember, gentlemen, in listening to her evidence, that, married to a drunken and violent husband, she has no power to get rid of him; for, as you know, another offense besides violence is necessary to enable a woman to obtain a divorce; and of this offense it does not appear that her husband is guilty."

Again Frome says: "If it please your lordship—Gentlemen of the Jury—My friend in cross-examination has shown a disposition to sneer at the defense which has been set up in this case, and I am free to admit that nothing I can say will move you, if the evidence has not already convinced you that the prisoner committed this act in a moment when to all practical intents and purposes he was not responsible for his actions; a moment of such mental and moral vacuity, arising from the violent emotional agitation under which he had been suffering, as to amount to temporary madness. My friend has alluded to the 'romantic glamour' with which I have sought to invest this case. Gentlemen, I have done nothing of the kind. I have merely shown you the background of 'life'—that palpitating life which, believe me—whatever my friend may say—always lies behind the commission of a crime. Now gentlemen, we live in a highly civilized age, and the sight of brutal violence disturbs us in a very strange way, even when we have no personal interest in the matter. But when we see it inflicted on a woman whom we love—what then?"

Such are the daily occurrences of life. It was this same psychological and biological knowledge that made Clarence Darrow one, if not the most powerful criminal lawyers.

Most of our criminal laws were written half a century ago and have been modified but little since. I have often been summoned to help decide whether the defendant is hopelessly insane or whether a verdict of only temporary insanity is possible. Think of the three questions that most courts ask expecting a "Yes" or "No" in answer. Did he commit this crime voluntarily and without compulsion? We as psychologists are not allowed to explain that millions of acts are performed under impelling ideas whether right or wrong. Joan of Arc goes down the pages of history as a heroine. But she was a monomaniac. There are plenty of situations in life which action in any direction might be pronounced wrong.

Who can ever tell any court even approximately what any given individual's "right mind" is without being permitted to explain? The whole procedure is antiquated and belongs to the dark ages. It is the hangover of our superstitions about sin and crime being fixed acts, and our perverted ideas about freedom and responsibility. Judge Olson of Chicago, who has handled over 40,000 criminals, points to medical evidence to show that a large part of high-powered crime is due to brain defects. Senator Copeland, chairman of the United States Narcotic Committee, attributes eighty to ninety per cent of the high powered crimes to narcotics. But the use of drugs of that kind is in turn due to physical and psychological abnormality.

The play *Justice* shows how a combination of even small events leads to a logical destiny. Just like the people and the papers today, the prosecutors in the play scoff at the plea of temporary insanity and call it a bizarre defense. Yet life is full of temporary insanity in any psychological sense of the term. Only the few are caught and brutally punished.

In one of many cases that I have known, a farmer of high reputation loaded his repeating rifle one morning, drove twenty miles alone over the plains to the home of a man who owed him some money. Some witnesses said he fired only one shot, others said two. When the farmer was questioned he said he had no knowledge of firing anything but the first shot which he thought was pointed to the ground. He also denied any knowledge of seeing the man slump down behind the wagon. But he admitted that he must have shot him and must have shot twice as empty shells indicated. When asked if the gun was fully loaded when he left home he said that it was: that he had loaded it to shoot rabbits and had no idea of seeing the man, much less of killing him. When asked if he fired the gun on the way, he said "no." Yet the court would not believe the testimony of a prominent neurologist that it was possible that he did temporarily lose consciousness or that the consciousness of the event might have been blotted out afterwards. So they sent him to prison for life.

Again, the keen analysis of this play shows how the relations of society make the innocent suffer as well as one punished. Some careful estimates indicate that on the average some four or five innocent people suffer for every one punished. The modern view does not, as its opponents foolishly suggest, claim that criminals should be turned loose any more than it claims that the insane should be. But it does hold that whatever we do should be done with the same attitude with which the wise physician treats his patients. Indeed Nietzsche was right when he said: "We shall no longer say pale criminal, but sick one."

THE PSYCHOLOGY OF COURT TESTIMONY: —The psychological difficulties of securing trustworthy evidence in court have been extensively investigated. The more we dive into the subject the more does the possibility of individual justice seem doubtful. Munsterberg was one of the first to give us a popular book on this subject, entitled *On the Witness Stand*. About this time extensive investigations were made in Europe by Jung and others. Gross published a volume of some 700 pages on *The Psychology of the Judiciary*. We have an English translation of this scholarly work. The most important aspect of all this is the difficulty of telling the truth even when you consciously desire to do so. Psychology for the most part discounts children's evidence. All evidence concerning color, dress, dates, and impressions resulting from great emotional excitement is uncertain even when it is the result of an honest effort to tell the truth. However, Munsterberg's book was not the first definite analysis of the witness stand. The first was Browning's *Ring and the Book,* published in 1868. Here we have a minute psychological analysis of court evidence. Here we have a great literary genius showing the detailed psychological and philosophical forces, both conscious and unconscious, that pervert the truth an individual is expected to tell— the impossibility of the truth, the whole truth, and nothing but the truth. It is a story told ten different times by ten different factions or individuals. No two of them agree. But the remarkable thing about the book is the causes why they do not agree. In the poem even dispassionateness is not trusted. Character alone becomes the criterion of truth, and even there psychological allowances must be made: individual acts merge into the social life of the people.

This tragedy is more than merely the disputed story of how Guido came to the brutal murder of his wife, Pompilia. It is life with all its conflicts, internal and external. In the first book we read:

> This was it from, my fancy with those facts,
> I used to tell the tale, turned gay to grave,
> But lacked a listener seldom; such alloy,
> Such substance of me interfused the gold
> Which, wrought into shapely ring therewith,
> Hammered and filed, fingered and favored, last
> Lay ready for the renovating wash
> O' the water. "How much of the tale was true?"

In the second book Guido solicits the sympathies of Half-Rome by posing as a wronged husband. This double life is prevalent everywhere. The third book—The Other Half-Rome would look beneath the surface and into the deep-seated causes. It shows sympathy with a suffering child-wife who came into her unfortunate situation through no fault of her own. It shows the absurdity of allowing a husband to be both judge and executioner. It turns out that Pompilia is not the daughter of Pietro. Yet he gave her dowery to Guido.

One court decision is thus set forth:

> "So answered Guido through the Abate's mouth.
> Wherefore the court, its customary way,
> Inclined to the middle course the sage affect.
> They held the child to be a changeling,—good:
> But, lest the husband got no good thereby,

They willed the dowry, though not hers at all,
Should yet be his, if not by right then grace—
Part-payment for the plain injustice done.
As for that other contract, Pietro's work,
Renunciation of his own estate,
That must be cancelled—give him back his gifts,
He was no party to the cheat at least!
So ran the judgment:—whence a prompt appeal
On both sides, seeing right is absolute.
Cried Peitro "Is the child no child of mine?
Why give her a child's dowry?"—"Have I right
To the dowry, why not to the rest as well?"
Cried Guido, or cried Paolo in his name:
Till law said "Reinvestigate the case!"
And so the matter pends, to this same day." [37]

But the story did not end there. The story is continued
by one who poses as neutral and who speaks for the upper
classes. In reality his chief object is to do credit to himself in the eyes of his listeners. With a great show of
cleverness both sides are presented. The whole impression
is lost in the show of neutrality. He finally concludes by
saying:

"Her Excellency must pronounce, in fine!
What, she prefers going and joining play?
Her Highness finds it late, intends retire?
I am of their mind: only, all this talk talked,
'T was not for nothing that we talked, I hope?
Both know as much about it, now, at least,
As all Rome: no particular thanks, I beg!
(You'll see, I have not so advanced myself,
After my teaching the two idiots here!)"

Next we find Count Guido striking out in his own
defense on the ground of the fraud perpetrated upon him

by the supposed father of Pompilia, and then of her elope-
ment. He and his sympathizers put the worst possible construction upon every act. Finally when he hears of the
birth of a child in the convent he commits murder as the
only means of vindicating his honor.

In the seventh book we have most powerful psychological material in the story of Pompilia as she lay dying in
the hospital. She knows she is dying, yet she is absolutely
self-possessed. She senses a notion of right and wrong
beyond that of public opinion and religion. Yet she for-
gives even the blackest of crimes against her. Her helpless
condition forced on her by others she excuses on psychological grounds without stating them as we do today.

The following quotations sound like one inspired:

> "All these few things
>   I know are true,—will you remember them?
>   Because time flies. The surgeons cared for me,
>   To count my wounds,—twenty-two dagger-wounds,
>   Five deadly, but I do not suffer much—
>   Or too much pain,—and am to die to-night."
> "On second thoughts, I hope he will regard
>   The history of me as what some one dreamed,
>   And get to disbelieve it at last:
>   Since to myself it dwindles fast to that,
>   Sheer dreaming and impossibility,—
>   Just in four days too! All the seventeen years,
>   Not once did a suspicion visit me
>   How very different a lot is mine
>   From any other woman's in the world.
>   The reason must be, 't was by step and step
>   It got to grow so terrible and strange."

This is sufficient to show any one the impossibility of
getting the truth, the whole truth, and nothing but the

truth from men and women who testify for or against their fellow man.

We have already said that most Russian writers from Tolstoy on have followed strictly psychological lines. Dostoievsky's *Crime and Punishment* is outstanding. One of the most striking conceptions in the book consists in the reactions of a college student who has committed a murder. The lawyer and magistrate who at least pretend a deep friendship for the murderer tell him he will rest better in prison after confession. This book is a storehouse of every form of conduct. It is the helpless plight of humanity—the terrible, the stupid, the wise, and the sublime are strangely mingled.

The whole modern attitude both in psychology and literature is one not of toleration, but of sympathy and pity. The modern attitude sees the shortcomings of man as mental and emotional diseases, not hopeless but to be treated as one treats bodily disease. The surgeon uses the knife when it is necessary even if it does cause pain. But he takes the course that will beget the best results and cause the least suffering.

We may not go so far as Tolstoy did and claim that we should forgive all criminals. But we do not yet know how far kindness and forgiveness will help to reform the offender. We do know that in spite of some failures and mistakes, the results so far have been better than any method yet tried. Most of the unfounded and half-baked criticisms are only echos from the dead past—or what should be dead.

"Judge not lest ye be judged, for with what judgment ye judge, ye shall be judged." "I say unto you forgive your enemies, not only seven times seven but seventy times seven."

CHAPTER XIV

MODERN RELIGIOUS PSYCHOLOGY
IN LITERATURE

MODERN PSYCHOLOGY EARLY attempted an explanation of
this world-wide phenomenon of religion. The explanation
of the Christians that saw God in their religion and the
devil in all others, soon crumbled under the power of
science and anthropological research.

In this country G. Stanley Hall began his psychological
study of religion as early as 1880. He met with vigorous
opposition. Religious conversion was a mystery: why attempt to explain it? But he pushed on, collecting facts of
all kinds. He soon showed that religious conversion
reaches its peak at the ages of sixteen or seventeen and
then declines. Why? What relation is there between the
maturing of adolescent emotions and religion? G. Stanley
Hall drew many parallels between love and religion. His
life work in this field culminated in his two volume edition of *Jesus in the Light of Modern Science*.

Prior to this James gave us his popular book on
Varieties of Religious Experience. He leads off boldly
with a chapter on *The Existential Value of Religion*.
Here he develops the idea that every religion must be
tested by its adaptability to serve the present needs of
humanity—irrespective of its origin or historic validity.
Then he gives us that pathetic side of religious life which
he calls the sin-sick soul. He shows the psychological
depths of despair. The other side of the picture is what

James calls healthy mindedness. In this chapter he gives a half dozen reasons for the growth of Christian Science and predicts that it will become a world religion. His chapter on Mysticism links religious mysticism with various other mental conditions. Indeed he suggests that the drunken man is in a state similar to that of the religious mystic—a state of affirmation and expansion that says "Yes" with unusual certainty.

Dr. Leuba has done much research on religion, chiefly from the standpoint of emotions. His first works were greeted with a sneer, for his opponents claimed that he had put the soul in the stomach. I have already said that religious dogma is one of the three great tragic delusions of the race. Certainly man is destined to sorrow as the sparks fly upward. How pathetic it is to think of the long history of the human race, trying to free itself from disease, from fear of death, from calamities, from a sense of guilt and consequent punishment, from invisible enemies, from its own sense of weakness and inferiority, from its own melancholy—by substitutions of the same nature and often many times worse than the original. The universal remedy for these emotional and intellectual distresses of mankind has always been some kind of religion in which fear and a sense of guilt, unworthiness and inferiority predominate. Intellectual Confucianism furnishes the only historic exception of any consequences. The two universal mysteries of man have always been and still are birth and death.

The history of this struggle of man for protection from physical disease, from fears, from his own sense of weakness and guilt, extends from savage days down to the most modern religious development. It is a great compromise with the realities of life. The instinct of self-elation will not permit us to admit our mental, moral, or physical limitations. These mental conflicts, centering

chiefly about moral conduct, are the chief causes of the
agony of the human race. After one has become his-
torically acquainted with this pathetic struggle and has
had the courage and scientific interest to observe all
forms of human conduct and to know personally a few
people belonging to all classes of society, the pathos of
it all cannot but awaken in him a profound sympathy for
man-kind. Especially are we distressed when we witness
the existence of crude survivals of barbaric religious performances in modern times along with our scientific development. Every now and then great spiritual leaders
beckon the race on to larger and better things only to see
it slipping backwards as time goes on. Before the World
War faith, hope, and courage seemed to point the way to
better things for humanity. But this catastrophe seems to
have swept the thinking classes away from even the most
liberal theology to no theology at all. How could any
theology satisfactorily explain the World War and its
consequences? On the other hand, with the masses of unthinking humanity, future fear, doubt, and uncertainty
have created a movement back to more primitive beliefs.

At the present time much is being said and written
about the disappearance of any religious attitude in high
school and college students. It must be admitted that we
have here one of our chief problems. But I wonder when
the majority of religious leaders will come to realize that
it is just the existence of these barbaric emotional out-
bursts, of these reactionary movements, of this gap between scientific progress and moral and religious progress
that produces this religious indifference. True, they do not
constitute a large part of our population, but they are an
important part. I wonder if religious leaders who con-
demn science, evolution, and modernism realize how completely they have lost this class of people. The so-called
"revolt of youth" is only an enlightened human nature

rebelling against a long dead past. The reactionary movements only prepare the rising generation to live in the dead past, instead of developing new and better institutions to meet their needs. Regressions and revolutions are produced by underlying forces of which the people are generally unconscious. Years ago Gumplowictz laid down this principle in his *Outlines of Sociology* and modern psychological study confirms this conclusion.

NEW ASPECTS OF RELIGION IN LITERATURE. The creators of great literature are the leaders of advanced thought in morals and religion. The plain facts stated by science have never proven so effective as the subtle suggestions of literature. These work reforms in human thinking which no other form of psychology can do. Here is a modern version of it by Lawrence Hope:

Unanswered

Something compels me, somewhere. Yet I see
No clear command in Life's long mystery.

Oft have I flung myself beside my horse,
To drink the water from the roadside mire,
And felt the liquid through my being course,
Stilling the anguish of my thirst's desire.

A simple want; so easily allayed;
After the burning march; water and shade.

Also I lay against the loved one's heart
Finding fulfillment in that resting-place,
Feeling my longing, quenched, was but a part
Of nature's ceaseless striving for the race.

But now, I know not what they would with me;
Matter or Force or God, if gods there be.

I wait; I question; Nature heeds me not.
She does but urge in answer to my prayer,
"Arise and do!" Alas, she adds not what;
"Arise and go!" Alas, she says not where!

Modern literature is dominated by an effort to widen and improve thinking along moral and religious lines. Indeed, this aim has never been absent in the best literature. It was the literary men of Greece, as we have seen, who held up to ridicule the idea of the gods quarreling. The advanced Hindu writers saw the biological problem of our time and expressed it in many ways.

Goethe put this truth best when he said:

"Bring pictures, but obscure their meaning.
A ray of truth through error gleaming.
Thus you the best elixir brew
To charm mankind and edify them too."

And we have already presented the keen sarcasm of Omar Khayyam on the religious dogmas of his time. Probably he has been most widely read.

Tolstoy occupies a unique place as a religious reformer. He early discarded all the miraculous and supernatural in religion, yet throughout his long life he maintained an uncompromising belief in the teachings of Christ, especially the Sermon on the Mount. He studied all religions—late in life he mastered Greek and Sanskrit to aid him in his search. Still he held the Sermon on the Mount to be the highest existent statement of moral law, and he declared that there could be no exception to a moral law. Forgive not only one minor offense, but the vilest of crimes.

In his *Diary* and *Confessions* he gives his own religious **transformation.**

"I read the whole of Rousseau. I was more than enthusiastic about him, I worshipped him. At the age of fifteen I wore a medallion portrait of him next my body, instead of the Orthodox cross. Many of his pages are so akin to me that it seems to me I must have written them myself."

Yet when he is 23 and with the army in the Caucasus, we find him struggling against vice, and, like a Faust, tossed to and fro.

"I wished to merge into the Universal Being. I asked Him to pardon my crimes; yet no, I did not ask for that, for I felt that if He had given me this blissful moment, He had pardoned me. I asked, and at the same time felt that I had nothing to ask, and that I cannot and do not know how to ask; I thanked Him, but not with words or thoughts. I combined in one feeling both petition and gratitude. Fear quite vanished. I could not have separated any one emotion—faith, hope, or love—from the general feeling. No, this was what I experienced: it was love of God, lofty love, uniting in itself all that is good, excluding all that is bad. How dreadful it was to me to see the trivial and vicious side of life! I could not understand its having any attraction for me. With a pure heart I asked God to receive me into His bosom! I did not feel the flesh. . . . But no, the carnal, trivial side again asserted itself, and before an hour had passed I almost consciously heard the call of vice, vanity, and the empty side of life. I knew whence that voice came, knew it had ruined my bliss! I struggled against it and yielded to it. I fell asleep thinking of fame and of women; but it was not my fault, I could not help it."

It was about this time that he wrote his first story—"Childhood."

He distinguished himself in the defense of Sebastopal, during the Crimean War. Shortly after this he was seized with the idea that dominated him the rest of his life and all his works. He wrote in his *Diary:*

"A conversation about Divinity and Faith has suggested to me a great and stupendous idea, to the realization of which I feel myself capable of devoting my life. This idea is the founding of a new religion corresponding to the present state of mankind: the religion of Christianity, but purged of dogma and mysticism: a practical religion, not promising future bliss but giving bliss on earth. I understand that to accomplish this the conscious labor of generations will be needed. One generation will bequeath the idea to the next, and some day fanaticism or reason will accomplish it. Deliberately to promote the union of mankind by religion—that is the basic thought which, I hope, will dominate me."

But Tolstoy had yet to pass through that awful religious struggle of four years, the outcome of which he describes as follows:

"I remember that it was in early spring: I was alone in the wood listening to its sounds. I listened and thought ever of the same thing, as I had constantly done during those last three years. I was again seeking God.

" 'Very well, there is no God,' " said I to myself. 'There is no one who is not my imagination but a reality like my whole life. He does not exist, and no miracles can prove his existence, because the miracles would be my perceptions, besides being irrational.' . . .

"But then I turned my gaze upon myself, on what went on within me, and I remembered that I only lived at those times when I believed in God. As it was before, so it was now; I need only be aware of God to live; I need only to forget him, or disbelieve in him and I die. . . . 'What more do you seek?' exclaimed a voice within me. 'This is he. He is that without which one cannot live. To know God and to live is one and the same thing. God is life.

Live seeking God, and then you will not live without God.' And more than ever before, all within me and around me lit up, and the light did not again abandon me." [38]

Tolstoy's genius has been displayed in his remarkable stories. The style is simplicity itself. In 1890 Thomas Y. Crowell and Co. printed the chief ones in a volume called *The Gospel Stories*. The two chief ideas of the new religion which Tolstoy hoped to inaugurate run through all of his stories: namely, that the good prevails in everybody, and that religion consists in living and doing good—not in beliefs, theories, ceremonies and creeds.

Human nature and a part of the human struggle is well presented in his *How Much Land a Man Needs*. A city sister visits the sister living in the country. Her comparisons and complaints produce dissatisfacton in the whole family. The devil suggests to Simon that he buy his neighbor's farm. They all save and work and buy one after another. But the more land they get the more trouble they have.

Finally the devil suggests to Simon that away down south live a foolish people who give away all the land any one wants—the best of wheat land. Simon travels many days and finds the people ready to satisfy him.

At sun rise Powhan's men assembled on a hill near by. Simon is told that at the firing of the gun he may start and that he may have all the land he can walk around from sun up to sun down. Men will follow him on horse-back and put down stakes.

He takes in the wealthy country. At the signal he plunges off at a running speed. He took in first one valley after another. In haste he ate a part of his lunch and threw the other away. At last he has turned for the home stretch. He sees the men on the hill. Soon he will be there. But the sun is low in the west. He went down in a valley. He could not see the sun. "But the sun," he said, "is shining on the hill." He threw away his clothes and made a desperate dash for the goal. But he fell to the ground. The blood gushed out of his ears and nose. And Powhan said to his men, "Bury him on a spot three by six. So much land a man needs."

When Tolstoy was seventy years old he produced his great novel *Resurrection*. It is in this monumental work above all others that he sets forth the tragic effects on even the best of people of habitually administering punishment to others. He also maintains that of all those punished no one is reformed. Gradual degeneration of those who are punished is the result. He presents in detail this semi-conscious degeneration. And dehumanizing effect on all who have part in the punishing. The work closes with the Sermon on the Mount.

In *Les Miserables* [39] the Bishop is the incarnation of Tolstoy's religion. Theories, churches, and ceremonies are put in the background. The Bishop even lies to save *Jean Valjean*. Society and lack of education are designated as the chief sources of crime.

Hugo was indulgent toward women and toward the poor, upon whom the weight of society falls most heavily; and said: "The faults of women, children and servants, of the feeble, the indigent, and the ignorant are the faults of their husbands, fathers and masters, of the strong, the rich and the wise." At other times he said: "Teach the ignorant as much as you can; society is culpable in not providing instruction for all, and it must answer for the night which it produces. If the soul is left in darkness, sins will be committed. The guilty one is not he who commits the sin, but he who causes the darkness."

Jean Valjean, the escaped criminal, is cared for and

fed by the Bishop. But he steals the silver and escapes with it. He is arrested the next day and taken back to the Bishop. The Bishop says he gave *Jean* the silver.

Jean Valjean opened his eyes and looked at the Bishop with an expression which no human tongue could describe.

When Churchill's *Inside of the Cup* [40] appeared it was possible even in Protestant churches to hear it praised by some and condemned by others. But it has done much to bring about modifications of religious thinking.

Hundreds of pieces of literature pointing in the same direction could be surveyed. When G. Stanley Hall declared as early as 1890 that most of our religion is insincere, honey-combed with hypocrisy, originating in the Orient, critics held up their hands in horror. Yet he gave us two large volumes on *Jesus in the Light of Modern Science,* in which His teachings are extolled above those of all men. But literature has poured forth volumes of still more penetrating criticism.

Almost every one of Ibsen's works takes thrusts at the dead ideals we pretend to believe in. He shows how they have lost all effect on conduct. Recall the arraignment of Pastor Manders towards the close of *Ghosts.* When the Master Builder's house burns down and the two children are lost, the next day his wife is lamenting, not the loss of her children, but of her ancient rugs and beautiful dolls. All through his popular work—*The Doll's House* runs a subtle current against ancient traditions of all kinds.

Helmer: To forsake your home, your husband, and your children! And you don't consider what the world will say.

Nora: I can pay no heed to that. I only know that I must do it.

Helmer: This is monstrous! Can you forsake your holiest duties in this way? . . . Before all else you are a wife and a mother.

Nora: That I no longer believe. I believe that before all else I am a human being, just as much as you are—or at least that I should try to become one. I know that most people agree with you, Torvald, and that they say so in books. But henceforth I can't be satisfied with what most people say, and what is in books. I must think things out for myself, and try to get clear about them.

Helmer: Are you not clear about your place in your own home? Have you not an infallible guide in questions like these? Have you not religion?

Nora: Oh, Torvald, I don't really know what religion is.

Helmer: What do you mean?

Nora: I know nothing but what Pastor Hanson told me when I was confirmed. He explained that religion was this and that. When I get away from all this and stand alone, I will look into that matter too.

TRANSITION STAGES IN RELIGIOUS THINKING. These extreme positions in modern literature have not been reached by a single bound. All things are a part of a great evolution in human thinking. In general the literature of any age has gone beyond the thinking of that age. So far as we can judge the 200,000 lines of *Mahabharata* reached far beyond the common thought of the Hindus at that time. It is one of the most beautiful and philosophical poems in all literature. We must either accept this far-reaching point of view or ascribe to that ancient nation a civilization beyond that of our own.

That the literature concerning Christ transcends His age, if not all ages, is universally true. It was for this that He was crucified. Christ was concerned primarily with what we now call the psychology of human relations. The absence of theory and philosophy is very marked. Even the statement that the Father and I are one may be conceived of as a philosophy that far transcends medieval theology. The parables of Christ peer into the future.

Is not the exhortation: "Ask and it shall be given unto you; seek, and ye shall find; knock, and it shall be opened unto you" what we know in modern psychology under the head of purpose? It is purpose, determination that has opened all the doors of humanity.

Only reflect on the far-reaching psychological penetration of the following statements:

"Judge not, that ye be not judged.

For with what judgment ye judge, ye shall be judged; and with what measure ye mete, it shall be measured to you again.

And why beholdest thou the mote that is in thy brother's eye, but considerest not the beam that is in thine own eye?

Or how wilt thou say to thy brother, Let me pull out the mote out of thine eye; and, behold, a beam is in thine own eye?

Thou hypocrite, first cast out the beam out of thine own eye; and then shalt thou see clearly to cast out the mote out of thy brother's eye.

Give not that which is holy unto the dogs, neither cast ye your pearls before swine, lest they trample them under their feet, and turn again and rend you.

Ask, and it shall be given you; seek, and ye shall find; knock, and it shall be opened unto you.

For every one that asketh receiveth; and he that seeketh findeth; and to him that knocketh it shall be opened.

Not every one that saith unto me, Lord, Lord, shall enter into the kingdom of heaven; but he that doeth the will of my Father which is in heaven.

Many will say to me in that day, Lord, Lord, have we not prophesied in thy name? and in thy name have cast out devils? and in thy name done many wonderful works?

And then will I profess unto them, I never knew you; depart from me, ye that work iniquity."

Milton's *Paradise Lost* and *Paradise Regained* must have a symbolic meaning or none at all. The author is in general orthodox, yet he evidently meant to go beyond the thought of his time. Near the close we read:

"True image of the Father, whether throned
In the bosom of bliss, and light of light
Conceiving, or remote from Heaven, enshrined
In fleshy tabernacle, and human form,
Wandering the wilderness, whatever place,
Habit, or state, or motion, still expressing
The Son of God, with godlike force endued."

Dante's *Divine Comedy* bridges a gap between the crude literal thought of early religion, and modern thought. When he comments on the souls who are rambling in the wilderness on the outskirts of Hell simply because they died without being baptized he is ridiculing the many strange ideas about this ceremony.

The fact that the drunkard, the licentious, and the spendthrift are punished in adjacent parts of Hell, while the passage to the abode of the miser is remote and difficult is not without a deep psychological meaning. Again, not only were many of the distinguished characters of the past found in Hell; but a few are mentioned who were then living. All this suggests that Hell is the tragic conflict of human emotions, and desires. Yet we find that the work recognizes a field into which human reason cannot penetrate. Here Beatrice symbolizes divine inspiration.

The scientific psychology of religion and the psychology expressed in modern literature are joining hands. Psychologists owe a debt to literature for its expansion of the psychology of religion and for that deep insight that often goes before and beyond scientific investigation.

CHAPTER XV

SEX PSYCHOLOGY IN LITERATURE

HERE WE ENTER into the most uncertain and disputed field in all psychology——the psychology about which there is least consistency in literature. I have already said that the three great tragedies of the human race are love, war, and religion. Each has claimed countless victims. But the greatest tragedies have been the millions that have lived through a lifetime, most frequently under cover from the eyes of the world. These secret sorrows, sufferings, and tragic conflicts are back of our interest in imaginary tragedy.

Sex psychology is one of the chief developments of modern science. Young and unreliable as it is, it has extended every field of thought, touching on human relations, medicine, and religion.

Scientific accuracy is next to impossible in this field. Not only is this due to the popular hedging on the subject but due chiefly to the fact that on this subject practically all men are liars.

This preface is chiefly in preparation for an understanding of many of our modern writers who touch on this subject. But it is chiefly Freudian sex psychology that has saturated literature for a quarter of a century. Freud's interpreters have ruined a really valuable contribution to modern science. The effort to carry this over into literature has only made things worse.

When Freud tries to found everything in the creative

urge—the *libido*—he does not mean sex in any popular sense of the word, but something much deeper and wider. In this respect it parallels Bentham. He invented the word *altruism* to cover not only conscious sacrifice, but the unconscious giving up of self for race. It is not unlike Weissman's biological doctrine that everything was wrapped up in the first germ cell of life, that the body cells exist only for the sake of the germ cells, and that the length of life depends upon the needs of the species. No one gets excited about this. Even Henry Drummond based his *Ascent of Man* on the idea that all things have developed out of two fundamental instincts—nutrition and reproduction.

However, the basis for the misinterpretation is found in Freud's doctrine of sex suppression. That sex suppression is universal and therefore normal from the general standpoint no well-informed individual will deny. All kinds of religious devices as well as others have been invented to produce and maintain this suppression as a means of proper sex control. To this sex suppression Freud chiefly attributes our dreams and many perplexing mental disorders. The suppressed effects of sex experiences and desires, plus the prominence given to the unconscious or subconscious, form the basis of psychoanalysis.

LITERATURE AND SEX. In a general way this topic might be considered from three angles. First, we have the great pieces of literature in which sex is treated under the form of love-emotion and the tragedies that come from these entangling emotions. Some of these writers touch the subject delicately, others indirectly. In the second place we have a few special and modern writers, such as Dostoievsky, Chekhov, Strindberg and Proust—who have assumed a purely psychological attitude and have to a large extent covered the whole of human life. Sex is developed and analyzed only as a part of man's original nature even though it is often considered the most powerful part. Finally we have the Freudian psychology carried over into literature where nothing is suppressed or even disguised and where Freudian principles are so poorly understood as to be perverted into a kind of a sex-religion.

STANDARD LITERATURE. Of course sex in some form could not be left out of any literature that has a universal appeal. In man, as well as in the world of nature sex and the reproduction of the race have been dominant elements in conduct. Millions of boys and girls who have no interest in formalistic study burn midnight oil to read almost any kind of literature that in some way stimulates the sex instinct. The delicacy with which sex is presented in Hindu literature is most outstanding. The moral tone of *Mahābhārata* and *Ramayana* is absolutely unsurpassed. Not only is this true, but the positive side of virtue is made dominant. To this day Hindu girls are led to look upon Sita[41] as the most perfect model of virtue and purity ever pictured in literature. Her wanderings during her banishment are all known and committed to memory. Indeed Rama and Sita are the Hindu ideals of a perfect relationship between man and wife. Rama is also an ideal ruler as thus expressed:

"For our humble wars and troubles, Rama bath a ready
      tear;
  To our humble tales of suffering, Rama lends his willing
      ear!"

No more subtle moral influence has ever been exerted in literature. And it is at least a reflection of the past life of the Hindus. Rama is about to be crowned king in the place of his aged father when the old nurse of Rama's stepmother poisons her mind and leads the stepmother to exact the fulfillment of a promise from the old king before telling him what the promise is. The subtle power of suggestion is used and thus described:

"Like a slow but deadly poison worked the ancient
    nurse's tears,
And a wife's undying impulse mingled with a mother's
    fears!"

When she gets the promise she calls for the banishment of Rama for fourteen years. Rama wishes to trust his wife *Sita* to his brother *Laksman*.

"Dearly loved, devoted Sita! daughter of a royal line,
Part we now, for years of wand'ring in the pathless
    woods is mine,

For my father, promise-fettered, the Kaikeyi yields the
    sway,
And she wills her son anointed,—fourteen years doth
    Rama sway,

But before I leave thee, Sita, in the wilderness to rove,
Yield me one more tender token of thy true and trust-
    ful love!

In our Bible there is a marked evolution from the Old Testament to the New. Tolstoy said that the immorality of the Old Testament was surpassed only by Shakespeare, especially in those works which the critics call his best. In a little book on Shakespeare he brought together some of these immortal passages. But it seems to me that he overlooks the fact that both the Old Testament and

Shakespeare are descriptions of the *whole of life at a given time in human development*. The same should be said of Homer's *Iliad*. Idealism, if introduced at all into these literatures, was very weak.

It is against this lack of idealism that Plato so strongly rebels. He, too, thought that it was disgraceful for Homer to paint the gods as licentious, quarrelsome, pugnacious, and deceitful. Not many of us would like to accept David as our present and future model even though he was painted as a "man after God's own heart."

The Old Testament seems to have considered that women exist for procreation and for man's sexual satisfaction. Indeed, the underlying assumption of some religions today is still this same conception. Some form of polygamy was taken for granted. It usually assumed the form of keeping concubines. But the movement for woman's rights is gaining ground.

In the book of Esther, however, the sex idealism is most significant. It is the index that has, as in the Hindu literature, always pointed to something higher than the animal and physical side of sex. Here the concubines are not absent, but there is evidence of that soul relationship that grows out of sex on a higher plane. When properly embodied in literature this relationship has always made an appeal.

The moral tone of Goethe's *Faust* is unquestionable. While sex dominates in the first part, yet it is handled in the most delicate manner possible. And the moral reaction is intense and even uplifting. The oft-repeated rebellion against his temptation is outstanding:

> Vile reprobate! go get thee hence;
> Forbear the lovely girl to name!
> Nor in my half-distracted sense,
> Kindle anew the smouldering flame!

From Ibsen's *When We Dead Awake,* I have already quoted the conversation between the Artist and his model who had left him ten years before. In lamenting her loss and trying to fathom the reason for her departure, the Artist asked if he had not always conducted himself properly when she acted as a model. She simply replies:— "That was the trouble—You were too inhuman."

The three great tragic writers that preceded Homer did not overlook even the biological place and power of the sex instinct. Aristotle gave it due recognition and gave us one of the best descriptions ever penned.

Plato's *Republic* gave birth to an idealistic attitude toward sex and has modified many pieces of literature. The so-called *New Thought* is largely founded upon it. In the *Republic* the sex instinct is to be shoved back into its original biological function—reproduction only. Even eugenics was to be put into practice. Only the wise rulers of the State could say who should have children. Then the children were to be raised by the State and never to know their parents. Weak and defective children were to be exposed.

Tolstoy, in one of his latest works, went beyond this and predicted a state of complete celibacy. Shortly before his death I had the pleasure of seeing him. When I questioned him about this, he simply smiled and said that he saw no harm in the ideal for even its existence would still leave plenty of opportunity for the propagation of the race. We have something of this same idealistic and Platonic modification and limitation in Churchill's *Far Country* and in Wells' *Men Like Gods.*

THE BROAD AND SPECIFICALLY PSYCHOLOGICAL WRITERS. Here the field is much larger than the special ones mentioned. Former chapters have already presented considerable material evidencing the degree to which Strindberg, Chekhov, and Dostoievsky entered into the significance of the creative urge and the social codes which have grown out of it.

I have already referred to G. Stanley Hall's development of abnormal psychology. But a quarter of a century before he published his discoveries the great Russian writer Dostoievsky began developing in literature almost every form of abnormal mental states. His knowledge in these lines is as difficult to explain as that of the mathematical genius. He not only describes the personality of these defectives and degenerates but he uses their language and shows their behaviour. He had, so far as we know, no access to such literature, nor could he have been acquainted with all these characters, even if he did understand his own defect, that of epilepsy.

In the chapter on abnormal psychology we shall return to this gifted psychologist. Here we are concerned chiefly with that part relating to certain sex abnormalities. Modern medicine has developed a whole literature relating to those individuals whose sex enjoyment seems to spring from suffering or inflicting pain. He makes one of his extremely hysterical characters say: "I should like some one to torture me, marry me and then torture me, deceive me and then go away. I don't want to be happy."

In his work called *The Possessed* Dostoievsky pictures the life of an unfortunate with the fundamental urge of life perverted until the full pleasure is possible only by suffering, or by inflicting pain and causing humiliation. What is greatest of all, Dostoievsky every where sees the biological, physiological, and psychological causes which drive the individual on to his destiny.

The perfect sinner *Staurogin* is urged by another abnormal defective to confess his many crimes but when his companion sees that he is not sincere and only intends to flaunt his sins in the face of God, he shouted out: "Poor, lost youth, you have never been so near another and still greater crime as you are at this moment. Before the publication of the Confession, a day, an hour perhaps before the great step, you will throw yourself on another crime as a way out, and you will commit it solely in order to avoid the publication of these pages."

Among the normal and well-balanced psychologists of modern literature Marcel Proust is outstanding. Although he introduces the modern view of sex and carefully analyzes its development, yet he does not overemphasize it.

In his work called *Swann's Way* the development of Swann's love for Odette occupies for the most part the center of interest. It is the growth and dissolution of a love affair in its psychological aspects. Swann is trying to forget Odette and tries to center his mind on a stronger woman whose picture he places on his table. But when Odette avoids him he is soon found searching the restaurants. Then follow these keen statements:

"Among all the methods by which law is brought into existence, among all the agents which disseminate this blessed love, there are few so effective as the great gust of agitation which, now and then, sweeps over the human spirit. For there the creature in whose company we are seeking amusement at that moment, her lot is cast, her fate and ours decided, that is the creature we shall henceforth love. It is not necessary that she should have pleased us up until then, any more or even as much as the others. All that is necessary is that our taste should become exclusive."

FREUDIAN PSYCHOLOGY IN LITERATURE. Dorothy Richardson is a modern Freudian writer. Through her novels, such as *Deadlock* and *The Tunnel,* she has commanded much attention. Everywhere in the background lie the unconscious and the censor of

Freudian psychology. Her chief characters are caught between instinct and good taste or custom. Mariam Henderson, one of her chief characters, rebels against the religion of tradition. This rebellion is expressed in one place as follows: "Woman is undeveloped man . . . if one could die of the loathsome vision . . . Sacred functions . . . highest possibilities . . . sacred for what? The hand that rocks the cradle rocks the world? The future of the race? What world? What race? Men . . . Nothing but men . . . forever?"

Katherine Mansfield and Rebecca West have attracted much attention by their sex psychology. Miss West in *The Judge* and *The Return of the Soldier* dives into sex abnormalities of the Freudian type. Miss West is a behaviorist and not a moralist. A worthless creature proposes marriage as follows: "Marion, I hope you understand what I am asking you to do. I am asking you to marry me. But not to be my wife. I am getting on in life, you see, so that I can make the promise with some chance of keeping it." Of course no one believed his lie but Marion.

Cummings in *The Journal of a Disappointed Man* leaves little to the imagination. Sex life underlies the whole work, but in the form of fears and repressions. He says: "I am capable of all the passions for I have them all within me."

D. H. Lawrence says: "We shall be free, freer than angels, ah, perfect." You need not read much to realize that but you may be disgusted. You will read many sex facts that have not been uttered elsewhere, even in writings classed as abnormal. Lawrence is often lost in the Freudian dream theory. But when he comes to a description of the abnormal relation between suffering and sex it is true to what medical science asserts.

This survey might be extended in all these fields. But

this will demonstrate the efforts of all classes of literature to deal with sex psychology. In this respect literature reflects the attitude of the age and of religion. With the modern scientific study of sex, literature will become more and more influenced by it. Sex psychology must depend upon literature for a wider knowledge than common observation can furnish. Its value stands next to that of medicine. G. Stanley Hall was right in collecting condemned books to widen his knowledge. We shall know little of the inner sex life in general so long as humiliating criticism and sexual taboo compel lying in every one.

The current prejudice against sex knowledge is to be regretted. But even authors whose enthusiasm or thirst for popular attention have led them to loose and even false statements have helped to overcome this prejudice.

True womanhood involves more than being a wife. Sex relation is brief. Sympathy and care of offspring is long and varied. The glorified madonna represents the highest conception. If any one thing in the world is more sacred than another it is the mother.

CHAPTER XVI

ABNORMAL PSYCHOLOGY IN LITERATURE

DEVELOPMENT OF ABNORMAL PSYCHOLOGY. As already stated, little was done in abnormal psychology until G. Stanley Hall gave impetus to the movement. Prior to that time the so-called abnormal were thought of as apart from general humanity: at one time all insane persons were looked upon as possessed of evil spirits. These ideas and beliefs, which are as old as the centuries, seem never to die. Even today many intelligent people feel disgraced if they are compelled to admit having an insane relative. We must begin to view these unfortunates known as abnormals in the proper scientific manner.

Until the close of the eighteenth century the insane were abused, mistreated, and grossly misunderstood. This condition of affairs grew so bad in France that the heroic Frenchman Philippe Pinel could stand it no longer. More than once did he risk his life in trying to reform the insane asylums of which he had charge. The city council of Paris refused to abolish the awful abuses which he pointed out. He replied by turning loose all the insane in his charge.

This awakened the people: reform was started which soon spread to England and Germany. We have now made great progress in the care and treatment of the insane, although to the Mohammedans belongs the honor of being the first people to be kind to them.

It remained for G. Stanley Hall to insist on the study of animals, savages, children, criminals, and the insane as the proper avenue to the understanding of the normal adult mind. In this expansive psychology lies the most comprehensive view of human life ever taken. Extensive material has accumulated in all these fields.

In dealing with delinquents, Healy, Goddard, and others have shed a world of light on human conduct. Mental conflicts have been clearly set forth. Psychopathology has made wonderful strides and the study of the insane has now become a first class science with an accumulation of facts not equalled in many sciences.

Of the many works on abnormal psychology Professor McDougall gave us in 1926 one of the sanest and most comprehensive. He treats drug-effects, hypnosis, dreams, Freudian theories, conflicts, complexes, dissociation of personality, fears, obsessions, sex perversions, hallucinations, mania, schizophrenia. Taylor's *Readings in Abnormal Psychology and Mental Hygiene* should be digested by writers who wish to deal with these subjects.

When literature represents the complete loss of past memories without other interruptions of the normal routine, or the abnormal recall of past memories, we do not need to question its possibility. We may doubt the advisability of presenting the horrible as Dostoievsky and Strindberg portray it, but we now know it to be a real part of human life and conduct. We know that such mental disorders are the result of factors fairly well understood. On the other hand when literature is filled with the superstitious psychology of the past it becomes our duty to expose such a perpetuation of ancient myths.

THE RIGHT-OF-WAY. A quarter of a century ago this was a widely read book. As a student of psychology I was repeatedly asked if the lapse of memory in Charley Steele is possible. Not only is it possible, but every detail of the description is sound psychology. I shall therefore outline the chief parts of this novel by Conrad because it is typical of what occurs in several pieces of literature.

The scene is laid in Montreal. Charley Steele has married a woman who was, before her marriage, interested in a certain Judge. Steele is a brilliant lawyer. Charley has been known all along as an independent thinker. He now takes to drink and becomes bolder in the expression of his opinions. This arouses strong persecution, especially among the Catholics. However, his reputation as a lawyer and public speaker constantly increases.

One day an old, unknown lumberman is arrested, charged with having killed a man up in the mountains. Charley Steele comes forth to defend him. When the time comes for him to speak, the expectant crowd is disappointed. He quietly reminds the Judge that no one saw him commit the crime, that the Old Man has not opened his mouth, and that no one knows his name nor whence he came. He points to the law that forbids condemning a man under such circumstances. The prisoner is freed. As he goes out he attempts to thank Charley Steele, who only replies: "Go out of my sight. You are as guilty as hell."

A few nights later at a drinking place Charley gets into a quarrel with a group of Catholics. The quarrel leads to the steep bank of the St. Lawrence. A blow on the head sends Charley down the embankment into the river. A man coming down the river on a raft sees the body and pulls it upon the raft. Slowly and after hours Charley regains consciousness. But he has no memory of the past. He goes with the Old Man to his lonely mountain home. There he lives, works, and clears land for ten years. The Old Man does not recognize Charley. He brings a priest from Quebec to baptize the stranger and administer the sacrament. Once he has tasted the wine, he is a changed man. In the night he steals what is left and gets drunk. The past speaks in powerful tones, yet he does not recognize it.

One day the Old Man had been to Quebec and brought home a newspaper wrapped around some packages. On the front page is a glowing description of the marriage of Mrs. Charley Steele to the Judge. It contains a full account of the mysterious disappearance of Charley Steele. Charley comes to himself and recognizes the entire past.

The emphasis in this novel is on this one abnormal phase of psychology which is far more common than is generally suspected. Several years ago a well-known biologist left Johns Hopkins University, went on board a boat to Boston, played games with people on the boat, registered at the hotel and on the third day came to himself, reading a newspaper. A teacher in Columbia University walked most of the way from Troy, N. Y. to Colorado Springs. He hired himself out at different occupations. After nearly two years he happened to be working for a man who was interested in reading scientific books. One day the man remarked that he had some books by Thorndike. The stranger laughed and said that he used to work with Thorndike. By degrees all his past came back to him. He recognized and identified his own picture put in the papers at the time of his departure. Later he wrote up his own story for one of our magazines.

Then we have the classic account of Dr. Hanna who was thrown from his carriage and later regained consciousness. But his memory of the past was so deeply buried that he had to learn everything anew. The first evidence of his past life was given when he complained of his two kinds of dreams—vivid ones and muddled ones. It was found that the first contained only material based on his life since the accident and the others related to life afterwards. Finally there was a conscious oscillation from one to the other. Finally, by skillful suggestion of his physicians he put the two together.

All the cases mentioned above except that of Dr. Hanna were perfectly normal save for the loss of memory. However, the hospitals and insane institutions contain many that do not behave thus. The loss of memory may be followed by extreme depression or some of the many forms of insanity. Dostoievsky describes in accurate detail several such cases. As we have already seen he is the master of abnormal psychology in literature.

Psychic epilepsy is a form of amnesia similar to somnambulism. The sleep-walker may climb down a dangerous fire escape, dodge street cars and automobiles and yet be asleep. Psychic epilepsy is a temporary loss of not only past but, in a way, of present consciousness, or at least of all but the *present moment*. The victim may drive an automobile through a city at an unlawful rate, and when he is arrested later have no consciousness of what he has done. Or he may commit an unusual and unexpected crime. The prisons contain more than one psychic epileptic. Hence these pictures of the loss of memory, of double personalities, and of abnormal memory power, as painted in literature are true to psychological facts universally agreed upon today.

On the other hand psychology is by no means ready to endorse mind-reading, thought transference, spiritualism, and so on, which are found in much of modern second-rate literature. Even Maeterlinck is continually suggesting these problems. His early writings are saturated with this tendency toward mind-reading, spiritualism, the mystical and supernatural. He lived in a twilight not justified by modern psychology—a twilight by no means free from that mystic religion which was then struggling to free itself from the New Realism.

Maeterlinck has become more scientific as our references to *The Blue Bird* demonstrate. His study of auto-suggestion, of hypnotism, of telepathy, and so-called psychic research led him into a mysticism differing from that of his early works. For example, in *Joyzelle* the different characters in the play are only multiple person-alities of the one leading character. In such a situation Maeterlinck is adhering to the scientific facts of abnormal psychology. Several cases of such multiple personalities are on record. Perhaps the most outstanding one is that of Doris Fisher of Boston. She was a high school girl who often manifested as many as seven different person-alities in a single day.

It appears that Maeterlinck made a specific effort to be scientific in this play *Joyzelle*. But in spite of this scien-tific leaning it must be admitted that the strongest appeal of most of Maeterlinck's work is made to those who want to believe in the mystic, in telepathy and spiritualism, in some sharp distinction between the natural and super-natural. The reasons for this appeal will become clear when we consider the philosophy lying behind his works. He said in one of his philosophic essays: "This is the road that leads from the seen to the unseen, from man to God, from the individual to the universe. At the end of the road lies hidden the general secret of life." Those who seek any agreement between modern scientific psy-chology and Maeterlinck's literature must not take too seriously his many implications of a supermind that works independent of the body and in supernatural ways.

The borderline between normal and abnormal mental states is so uncertain that it is easy to overlook their absolute relation and common origin. Abnormal psychol-ogy treats of the unusual phases of mental life, such as automatic writing, trances, hallucinations, number forms, hypnotism, sexual perversions, dreams, ecstasy, the "sin-sick soul," fixed ideas, and the various forms of insanity.

There are also marked disorders of all the mental powers, such as the disorders of memory, imagination, volition, feeling. Every one of these phenomena is in some degree represented in what we call normal life. Thousands of abnormal experiences are concealed by the so-called normal individual from others and from his physician. There is no fixed line between sanity and insanity, between hallucinations and powerful mental images, between illusion and faulty observation, between enthusiasm and ecstasy, between seriousness and melancholy, between consciousness of wrong and the "sin-sick soul." In most cases it is simply a question of intensity and complexity. Whatever line we fix is for the sake of convenience and is perfectly arbitrary.

The disorders of perception are manifested chiefly in the form of illusions and hallucinations. The interpretations of external stimuli may vary from the simplest inaccuracy to the wildest conceivable distortions. Illusions have some recognizable external stimuli; hallucinations have none. This distinction is not always clear; there are often mixtures of internal and external stimuli. The childish fantasy that sees all manner of faces in the clouds, and the imagination that fills your room with images of your dead friends are not widely separated. Such disorders as illusion and hallucination belong chiefly to the perceptions of sight and hearing. The degree of these disorders corresponds to the powerful and convincing influence which they have on the entire mental attitude of the individual.

The disorders of memory are many. We have several treatises on the diseases of memory. The first condition of a good memory is impressibility. When disturbances of this function exist, stimuli that act quickly are likely to leave no trace of their existence, and others are inadequately apprehended. These disorders often exist temporarily as a result of fatigue or illness; they are marked in dementia and in epileptic insanity. Accuracy of memory is only relative, but in morbid cases the past is always falsified. Hallucinations concerning the past seem the most real of all mental experiences.

Paramnesia is a term applied to a mixture of invention and reality. Some time ago a seventeen-year-old boy, in high school, apparently lost all power of orientation. He started out to visit a neighbor and became unconscious of his personal identity, relations, and location. He even traveled to different cities in this condition, but he was perfectly sane in every other way.

Paralysis of thought occurs in a mild degree as a result of extreme fatigue or of narcotics in poisonous doses. It is one of the symptoms of mental deterioration and senile dementia. Often there is quite a noticeable retardation of thought, even where there is no lack of mental ability.

Compelling ideas are those that seem to force their way into consciousness so as to produce a feeling of subjugation to some outside force. The fear of their return is often sufficient to enthrone them in consciousness. They usually accompany some emotional disorder, such as melancholia. The simple impulse to count or to ask one's self all sorts of questions is of a similar nature. When these *compelling ideas* remain for some time to harry the life of the individual, they are called fixed ideas. Most normal persons have periods when this disorder manifests itself in some form. Delusions are false beliefs which do not yield to argument or experience.

Volumes might be written on morbid emotions. The secret experiences of most individuals will furnish material out of which they may form conceptions of morbid emotions. Fear is the most common of emotional disorders, and accompanies nearly all mental disturbances. Its effect on the whole physical and mental organization is serious. Compelling ideas often take the form of some foreboding or fear.

In some of these abnormal states all sensitiveness to physical pain is lost. In extreme cases the individual may cut out his own tongue, destroy his eyes, etc., and remain insensible to pain.

DOSTOIEVSKY. Now let us return to the master psychologist in literature—to the man who demonstrated an almost incredible knowledge of abnormal psychology— to the man who stripped himself of all dogmas of the past and consciously plunged into the scientific description of life in such a way as to make his works live for centuries to come.

This genius was born more than a hundred years ago in Moscow. Yet he prophesied and described our new interpretation of human conduct, of morals, and of the new social order. He showed us the deplorable, helpless, and pitiable side of human life.

He was himself an epileptic and suffered from hallucinations. But that did not give him the key to all such abnormalities as mania, depression, melancholy, hysteria, dementia praecox, paranoia, obsessions, alcoholism, degeneracy or moral insanity. He studied every form of perverted humanity from the three-fold standpoint of the physical and biological, of the mental, and of environmental. He keeps a sane balance between the physical and mental. Despite whatever he may have felt and suffered himself he writes like a physician describing his patients.

What psychologist can better describe a confirmed hysteric than did Dostoievsky in these words: "I should like some one to torture me, marry me and then torture me, deceive me and then go away. I don't want to be happy."

And listen to this description of the psychopathic individual: "An unstable balance of the psychic impulses, an overfacile tendency to emotion, an overswift interchange of mental phases, an abnormally violent reaction of the psychic mechanism. The feature most striking to the beholder in the character of such sufferers is its heterogeneous medley of moods and whims, of sympathies and antipathies; of ideas in turn joyous, stern, gloomy, depressed and philosophical; of aspirations at first charged with energy then dying away to nothing. Another feature peculiar to these sufferers is their self-love. They are the most naive of egoists; they talk exclusive and persistently and absorbedly of themselves; they strive always to attract the general attention, to excite the general interest and to engage everyone in conversation concerning their personality, their ailments, and even their vices."

In *The Idiot* he makes one of his characters describe in the most detailed way the onset of an epileptic attack: "He thought amongst other things how in his epileptic condition there was one stage, just before the actual attack, when suddenly in the midst of sadness, mental darkness and oppression his brain flared up, as it were, and with an unwonted outburst all his vital powers were vivified simultaneously. The sensation of living and of self-consciousness was increased at such moments almost tenfold. They were moments like prolonged lightning. As he thought this over afterward in a normal state he often said to himself that all these flashes and beams of the highest self-realization, self-consciousness and 'highest existence' were nothing but disease, the interruption of the normal state. If this were so, then it was by no means the highest state, but, on the contary, it must be reckoned as the very lowest. And yet he came at last to the very paradoxical conclusion: What matter if it is a morbid state? What difference can it make that the tension is abnormal, if the result itself, if the moment of sensation when renumbered and examined in the healthy state proves to be in the highest degree harmony and beauty, and gives an unheard-of and undreamed-of feeling of completion, of balance, of satisfaction and exultant prayerful fusion with the highest synthesis of life? If at the last moment of consciousness before the attack he had happened to say to himself lucidly and deliberately 'for this one moment one might give one's whole life,' then certainly that one moment would be worth a lifetime. . . ."

At the close of our Civil War he published his most widely known work—*Crime and Punishment*. The following words describe the poor, helpless condition of one of his criminals: "If there is a will beyond my own, it must be an evil will because pain exists. Therefore I must be an evil to be in harmony with it. If there is no will beyond my own, then I must assert my own will until it is free of all check beyond itself. Therefore I must will evil."

Herbert Spencer looked upon pleasure in pain as inexplicable. In *Crime and Punishment* we find delight in all kinds of disgraceful conditions: "Every unusually disgraceful, utterly degrading, dastardly, and above all, ridiculous situation in which I ever happened to be in my life, always roused in me, side by side with extreme anger, an incredible delight."

From writings published after the death of Dostoievsky it appears that he had made plans for his masterpiece—*The Life of a Great Sinner*. The chief character was to contain all the Seven Deadly Sins of the Catholic Church, for the punishment of which Dante provides in the *Inferno*. What a marvellous relation he would have shown between the passions! He had already shown the minute mental relation between suffering, sex, anger, jealousy, and envy. In many places Shakespeare shows us the maddening power of jealousy. But no one but Dostoievsky goes into the minute analysis of jealousy such as is presented in *The Brothers Karamazov*.

The reader is likely to say: "Why trouble ourselves

with these exceptions in life? Why not let them pass off the stage of human action unnoticed?" But the sad fact is that they are by no means rare, as one investigation after another shows. Indeed many of the so-called sex abnormalities may turn out to be normal—belonging to the majority. Criminal mental tendencies constitute the chief problems of humanity. They modify our whole philosophy of life. But the thing which most concerns us is the fact that we do not know when we may be subject to them ourselves. In all things we have only relative stability. No one knows positively that he will not die in disgrace, in the penitentiary or in the insane asylum.

Many prominent men have lived on the ragged edge of crime or insanity. The life of Anthony Trollope is most pitiful. When he was nineteen, he says, he had "been plagued more than any human being alive." General Gordon is described as given to outbreaks that often made him the terror of his superiors. One Sunday he broke 27 panes of glass by shooting screws through them. The famous Goethe rambled in the woods for days on the verge of despondency and insanity. The world-famed Beethoven was subject to violent fits of anger in which he behaved like a child. It was at the age of twenty-seven and in one of these fits of anger that he lost his hearing. St. Theresa in the sixteenth century had cataleptic fits and was given to hysterical outbreaks. She often changed her confessor and had various hallucinations. So we might fill pages and pages of abnormal incidents from history even without entering the fields of sex and crime.

Modern writers such as Dostoievsky, Proust, Gorki, and Strindberg have done a great service to humanity and to the science of psychology. Indirectly they enable us to understand ourselves. Their insight into human conduct has pointed out a future for humanity. They have freed human thinking from the chains of dogma about the causes of human conduct.

CHAPTER XVII

SOCIAL PSYCHOLOGY IN LITERATURE

DEVELOPMENT OF SOCIAL PSYCHOLOGY:
Modern social psychology was born in the comprehensive
brain of Herbert Spencer. Centuries before him, Aristotle
had maintained the existence of a social instinct. Goethe
and other writers had pointed out the influence of this
natural tendency. But Spencer's two volume edition of
Sociology specifically followed psychology and developed
the doctrine of super-organic evolution. He saw clearly
the struggle for existence on the one hand and the social
compromise on the other. He prophesied a gradual evolution towards the latter.

Social psychology has developed along three distinct
lines. (1) We have those who like Spencer have emphasized the two factors of heredity and environment with
about equal intensity. They have seen social life as an
adjustment of internal relations to external conditions.
(2) A second class has placed the emphasis almost ex-
clusively on environment. (3) Still a third class has
placed the emphasis on the inherited biological impulses
or urges, operating through the semi-conscious or unconscious mind. All three have looked upon the development
as a super-organic or mind evolution.

To the Spencer class belong such writers as Geddings,
Ellwood, Hayes, Davis, Allport, McDougall, and G. Stanley Hall. These and many other writers look upon our
social institutions as the joint product of human instinct

and conditions. Nearly forty years ago Hall accumulated data and wrote on instincts and social institutions. Of course all modern writers have recognized these two factors. But they have differed as to where they place the chief emphasis. Indeed it was the extremely loose use of the word *instinct* in sociology and social psychology that in a measure drove psychologists such as Watson to behaviorism.

(2) Le Bon's *Psychology of the Crowd* emphasized environment and the power of suggestion in the determination of social conduct. After G. Stanley Hall, one of the earliest American productions was Ross's *Social Psychology*. It was this book that caused him to be dismissed from Leland Stanford University. He has written many works since then, but the emphasis is always on environmental conditions. Imitation, prestige, and suggestion are made to stand out. Bogardus has been a very popular writer on social psychology and follows essentially the same lines as Ross.

(3) The outstanding fact about the third class is the emphasis placed on heredity and the unconscious evolutionary mind forces. Early in the development Gumplowicz, in his *Outlines of Sociology,* conceived society as pushed on by underlying mental and instinctive forces, the operations of which we are largely unconscious until retreat is practically impossible. Then we begin to reason and speculate about them. As an illustration we may say that from the time the World War started, many forces began to stimulate and set in action the instinctive forces that finally declared themselves in 1917 and led us irresistibly into the most horrible and senseless war ever waged. Yet from every direction our reason hastened to its justification. In other words according to this writer the real causes of events are, as a general rule, detected only after the events have passed.

Ward's *Dynamic Sociology* is a further demonstration of these deep biological and psychological forces. Trotter's *Instinct of the Herd* points in the same direction. Henry Drummond, in his *Ascent of Man,* tries to trace all social and anti-social activities to the two original instincts of nutrition and reproduction — self-ism and other-ism. Weissman—the German biologist—considered every potentiality as having been wrapped up in the original germ cell of life. Or as Omar Khayyam put it: "With earth's first Clay they did the last Man knead."

Coaley's *Human Nature and the Social Order* is a psychological consideration from the standpoint of original nature. Wallas, in *The Great Society* seeks the deep underlying forces of society and their relationships.

As early as 1895 Benjamin Kidd created a profound sensation with his book on *Social Evolution.* He recognizes the struggle for existence. Yet he sees that the struggle must be softened to permit higher evolution. He holds that human reason is selfish and that only altruistic feelings can reduce the struggle. The purpose of all religions has been to produce an accumulated fund of altruistic feeling. This force will ultimately place all people on an equal footing in the struggle. The meaning of present events is found only in generations yet unborn.

THE ECHOES IN MODERN LITERATURE. These different aspects of social psychology are reflected in literature—especially the modern drama. The former chapters already contain much material on these lines. Ibsen's social dramas aim directly at these problems. The desire for individual freedom in this network of social causes seems to be Ibsen's chief problem. It shows itself everywhere in treating the social problems of marriage. But nowhere is it more dominant than in *The Lady from the Sea.*

Ellida: Oh, you must not think that, Wangel! I have had from you all that any one could possibly desire. But I did not come into your home of my own free will—that is the thing.

Wangel: (Looks at her) Not of your free will?

Ellida: No; it was not of my own free will that I cast in my lot with yours.

Wangel: (Softly) Ah, I remember—the phrase he used yesterday.

Ellida: The whole secret lies in that phrase. It has thrown a new light on things for me; so that I see it all now.

Later the conversation continues on the same line:

Ellida: Yes, yes—you must let me! I can assure you there will be nothing else for it in the end— after the way we two came together.

Wangel: (Controlling his emotions) So it has come to this!

Ellida: It had to come to this; no other end was possible.

Wangel: (Looks sorrowfully at her) So even in our daily life together I have not won you. You have never, never been wholly mine.

Ellida: Oh Wangel—if only I could love you as I gladly would! As tenderly as you deserve! But I feel quite clearly—it will never be.

Wangel: A divorce then? It is a divorce—a formal, legal divorce—that you want?

Ellida: My dear, you do not understand me at all. It is not the forms that I care about. These external things seem to me to matter nothing. What I wish is that we two should agree, of our own free will, to release each other.

Now the conditions become more intense as each demands a choice:

Ellida: I do not want to take refuge in the plea that I
am another man's wife—or that I have no
choice left me. For then my decision would decide nothing.

Wangel: You talk of choice! Choice, Ellida! Choice in
this matter!

Ellida: Yes, choose I must—freely choose either course.
I must be free to let him go away alone—or—
to go with him.

This problem of freedom in a complex society shows
itself in *Love's Comedy,* in *The Doll's House,* and in
Pillars of Society. It is intimately related to the problem
of getting rid of pretense, sham, and hypocrisy, which we
have already seen in *An Enemy of the People* and in
Pillars of Society.

Every social psychology struggles with the problem of
freeing man from the past. It is a practical problem of
social psychology, especially during transition periods such
as the one in which the world is now. But change that
leaves out the past is chaos. In this struggle Isben was a
pioneer. It seems to have been his chief problem. The true
significance of "Ghosts" appears near the close in the
speech of Mrs. Alving to Pastor Manders.

"Mrs. Alving: I ought never to have concealed the
facts of Alving's life. But . . . in my superstitious awe
for Duty and Decency I lied to my boy, year after year.
Oh! what a coward, what a coward I have been! . . .
Ghosts! When I heard Regina and Oswald in there, It
was as though I saw the Ghosts before me. But I almost
think we are all of us Ghosts, Pastor Manders. It is not
only what we have inherited from our father and mother
that "walks" in us. It is all sorts of dead ideas, and life-
less old beliefs, and so forth. They have no vitality, but
they cling to us all the same, and we can't get rid of them.

. . . There must be Ghosts all the country over, as thick as the sand of the sea. And then we are, one and all, so pitifully afraid of the light." [42]

Social psychology is always confronted with the question of what the real psychological difference is, if any, between the so-called upper and lower classes. Many efforts have been made to discover the inner make-up of the two classes. But no one has dealt so directly to this problem as Strindberg, in his *Countess Julie*.[43] He is almost brutally frank in laying bare the inner thoughts of these classes and analyzing to the bottom this age-long antagonism. He strips all the characters of all sham and pretense and shows their inner moral natures to be essentially the same.

"Countess Julie" is a one-act tragedy. Julie inherited the primitive, intense passions of her mother; but at the same time she is dominated by the aristocratic tendencies of her father. But she, in due time, feels the call of the wild. When the Count is absent and they are having a celebration she mingles freely with the servants. "All are in a holiday spirit, full of gladness, and rank is flung aside." Once having seen and tasted the freedom and abandonment of the common people, she soon realizes that their separation is only artificial and superficial, that it is due to nothing but their arrogance, to blind conceit and ignorance of humanity. Her long suppressed passions leap into flame. She throws herself into the arms of her coachman; not because she loves him or for sex; but simply because she is carried away by the new idea of freedom.

What real student of humanity, if he has mingled with all classes, has not detected that the so-called leaders of religion, of finance, of society, of politics, and even of learning are found to be about on a level with the masses so far as morals are concerned. Yet only the fiction writers dare to say so. It is almost a shock to the psychologist to learn how much ignorance and how little real thinking he finds among these classes.

Nowhere do we have such grim sarcasm on our conservative educational system as that presented by the German writer Frank Wendekind in his *The Awakening of Spring*.[44] A really gifted boy is expelled from school for his essay on the mystery of life.

Le Bon gave us a popular and valuable work on *Mob Psychology*. Galsworthy gives us *mass psychology* in his *Strife*.[45] It is even more stirring than the *Weavers*. It certainly describes the psychology of our present situation. Here we have John Anthony, president of the company, cold and conservative, yet honest and sincere. On the other side is the hot-headed revolutionist whose reason is blinded by heated emotions. Between are the strikers.

He says: "You don't want to hear me then? You'll listen to Rous and to that old man, but not to me. You'll listen to Sim Harness of the Union that's treated you so *fair;* maybe you'll listen to those men from London. . . . You love their feet on your necks, don't you? . . . Am I a liar, a coward, a traitor? If only I were, ye'd listen to me, I'm sure. Is there a man of you here who has less to gain by striking? Is there a man of you that had more to lose? Is there a man among you who has given up eight hundred pounds since this trouble began? Come, now, is there? How much has Thomas given up—ten pounds or five or what? You listened to him, and what had he to say? "None can pretend," he said, "that I'm not a believer in principle—but when Nature says: 'No further,' 'tis going against Nature!'"

We might extend this survey indefinitely by diving into the psychology of Hugo, Shaw, and many recent writers. But this should be sufficient to make us respect the contri-

butions of literature to social psychology. William Butler
Yeats' *Where There is Nothing* [46] is a fair interpretation
of the philosophy behind lawlessness and anarchy. The
careful psychological student of the times shudders for
fear we are on the road to this state of affairs.

RHESUS BY EURIPIDES. This tragedy, representing an episode in the Trojan War, is dominated by the
war instinct and the common deceptive arts and mistrust
that goes with war. The way in which everyone is dominated by the war spirit and the certainty with which each
holds his war to be just and that of his enemies unjust,
are psychological facts of modern interest and true to
human nature today.

PSYCHOLOGY OF DECEPTION. To accomplish
ends by means of deception has always been one of the
main arts of war. This play opens with Hector's excitement about the fires in the enemies' camps. He believes
that they are about to set sail for Greece and wishes to
fall upon them at once. But the armies persuade Hector
to send a spy into their camps. Dolon goes disguised as a
wolf. In the meantime a countryman arrives to announce
that Rhesus and his hosts are coming to help Hector.
Hector's jealousy and suspicion are aroused at once.
However, when he learns that Rhesus could not possibly
have come earlier Hector gladly accepts his support.
While Rhesus sleeps inside the Trojan camp, Dolon is
killed, the pass word is secured from him and Odysseus
and Diomedes from the Greek camp steal into the Trojan
camp, murder Rhesus, and steal his white horses. When
this foul murder is made known, the blame is placed on
Hector and he is charged with the treachery of a villain.
From a psychological viewpoint it is interesting to note
that the same kind of deception prevailed among the gods.
Indeed, it is by means of their deception that man suc-
ceeds. It is also true that this treachery and deception is

praised by those in whose favor it is performed, and is unreservedly denounced by the enemy.

We have now a great number of books on custom and imitation. Some of them attempt to show that custom is the fundamental principle by which society can be explained. Custom and imitation are presented as the main sources for the spread and perpetuation of social conduct and beliefs. Custom carries on many social ceremonies and institutions long after intelligence has outgrown them.

The various works of sociology have recently absorbed much of the psychology of custom. Here it is seen to be largely an unconscious force which holds on to old beliefs and conduct and which restores much of the past after revolutions. This force is all the more powerful because it is not generally felt, and the intellect constantly attempts to assume a rational explanation.

Also such books as Wells' *Outline of History* and Robinson's *Mind in the Making* approach the problem from another angle. They would explain social institutions and the continuity of history largely as the results of imitation and custom. Rationalization is our method of justification.

Only a few creative thinkers are able to rise above this power of custom. Most of what passes as reasoning or rationalizing about human relations is only the unconscious power of custom trying to maintain the present order of things. Thus we see that the psychology of custom has come to play an important place in scientific thinking.

CUSTOM IN LITERATURE. Our problem now is "To what extent did great writers discern this fact?" In some way, nearly all great pieces of literature deal with this problem. The early writers did so largely unconscious of any such principle as a rule of conduct. Later ones have caught the psychological atmosphere and are making definite use of the principle.

In Goethe's *Faust,* Wagner is typical of the people, bound hand and foot by custom. He says:

> "Let not this thought (custom) your soul ov'r cast.
> Can man do more than with nice skill
> With firm and conscientious will
> Practice the art transmitted from the past."

HOMER'S ILIAD. Perhaps no other work so definitely summed up the customs of a people as did the *Iliad.* It crystallized them into a bible. It gave definite form to the religion of a great people.

All these customs are woven about a comparatively small event, as viewed from the vantage point of modern times. When the book opens a war has been in progress against Troy for ten years. The war is to recover the beautiful Helen—stolen by Paris. The whole list of events recorded is crowded into the short space of forty-five days. The great themes of love, war, and religion are marvellously interwoven.

The customs may be summarized in definite outline:

1. Custom as to the relation of gods and mortals.
2. Customs of war down to the details of trenches.
3. Religious rites and funeral customs.
4. The customs of courtship, love, and marriage.
5. Social differentiations and customs of prestige.
6. A complete record of the customs of play and sport activities.

Few books show such an enumeration of customs and such a respect for them. The position and customs of the gods are clearly drawn. But even the gods sometimes trespass upon the boundaries of custom and are reprimanded for doing so. The chief of the gods thus admonishes Venus:

Not these, O daughter, are thy proper cares,
Thee milder arts befit, and softer wars
Sweet smiles are thine, and kind endearing charms;
To Mars and Pallas leave the deeds of arms.

The center of the entire work is the wrath of Achilles. Offended by Agamemnon who has seized his bride, he sulks apart from the Greeks until his friend Patroclus is slain. Then his wrath is unbounded. He engages in combat even with the gods.

But now the funeral rites must be performed. All the ancient rites are set in order for the funeral of Patroclus. Achilles sacrifices many animals and Trojan captives. The funeral games and contests are observed. Achilles says:

"Ere yet from rest or food we seek relief,
Some rites remain, to stop our rage of grief."

We have a complete recital of the famous games, chariot races and athletic contests, with prizes and honors. Few ever portrayed the habits and customs of a people so completely or accurately.

In conclusion we have one final comment on this long dispute concerning the relative influence of environment and heredity. It runs through literature, psychology, and education. Especially has the hasty social reformer swallowed the strong suggestions of social psychology and sociology concerning the dominance of environment.

The reformer, usually knowing nothing of biology, ignores her laws. Only change environment to suit their idealistic plans and they would make humanity over.

This idealism is being tried on a large scale in many countries and to no small degree in our own country. However, we can never hope for any fundamental modification of human nature that made the very environment which these idealistic reformers would throw overboard.

I have never understood why no one has seriously asked what made the environment? The manifestations of the sex instinct reign through all time and in all places. Investigations show that the varying manifestations have not been so great as many are inclined to think. Even John Stuart Mill said that the morality or immorality of the race is a fairly constant thing. Of course religion and various other forces do produce modifications but nothing fundamental. But religion is itself a universal phenomenon due to human nature—not the result of an accident.

Fighting and war make and maintain nations. In the development of the race this animal instinct got wrapped up with so many natural tendencies that we now stand amazed at its dominance over our reason and common sense. Any war today plays on the powerful tendencies or instincts of pugnacity, of fear, of hate and rivalry, of greed and gain, of self-preservation, and of the instinct of self-elation.

Even the savage struggles to possess something he calls his own, and to plunder others for more. If Russia or any other country thinks that she will blot out the instinct to possess this world's goods she is only deluded. The instinct of self-elation is also tied up with it. On the other hand we must admit the sad fact that we are always and everywhere confronted with large groups of humanity whose chief concern is food, shelter, and sex, and they do not work even for these unless it is necessary. Human laziness will never be cured by the dole.

So when we say that each generation is swallowed up by its environment that is only because the fundamental trend of conditions gives some social modification to these universal tendencies and impulses. Property laws differ in different countries, but they exist everywhere. Human nature made the fundamental trend of all environments.

CHAPTER XVIII

PHILOSOPHY IN LITERATURE

THIS SURVEY WOULD seem incomplete without some suggestions concerning the philosophical ideas behind great world literature—the very life blood of the race.

The sum of all philosophy is found in the three questions: What? How? Why? The What? How? Why? have helped to originate all religions from the crudest to the highest. The primitive religions have their mythical answer. All developed religions have added to their ceremonies some theological answer to these questions. The philosophical systems of India and of Greece attempted an answer to these problems. These systems in some form have modified and saturated all forms of thinking ever since. Literary writers are no exception.

Perhaps these questions were never asked so persistently and by so many people as they are today. Never did they receive such uncertain and agnostic answers. Independent thinking and the uncertainty of this age make it stand apart from all other ages. Whether right or wrong modern drama has done much to bring about this intellectual development. But greatest of all is the development of the scientific world. As the limits of knowledge are approached in any science a philosophy naturally develops. Many scientists attempt to avoid speculation, but few of the better thinkers succeed.

WHAT IS PROGRESS? Most modern literature aims at something called Progress. Such a destiny may be definitely or indefinitely conceived. It may be outstanding or in the background. It may be only a faith, a hope, or a philosophy.

Some writers are said to write only to please the public, to have no philosophy and no other desire. That has been said specifically of Shakespeare. Goethe once said: "I do not know why I write, I prefer that the principle from which and through which I write should be hidden from me."

But it must be admitted that there is only one way to "please the public" and that is by appealing to their psychological make-up. When the public has been pleased its deepest psychological nature has been touched.

On the other hand as Goethe once said:

"Bring pictures, but obscure their meaning.
A ray of truth through error gleaming.
Thus you the best elixir brew
To charm mankind and edify them too."

This is the highest art of all literature. The best literature of all ages has pointed to something beyond what the masses possessed. This is true even where the prevailing conditions were generally accepted. This impulsive struggle for change is a part of evolution. But for the literary writer progress is like tomorrow: "It always is becoming and never is."

Browning expresses it admirably in *A Death in the Desert*.

"Progress, man's distinctive mark alone,
Not God's and not the beasts': God is, they are;
Man partly is, and wholly hopes to be."

Until recently democracy was hailed as the god of

progress. No one expresses this better than Mr. Bury in his *Idea of Progress.*

"The earthly progress of humanity is the general test to which social aims and theories are submitted as a matter of course. The phrase *civilization and progress* has become stereotyped, and illustrates how we have come to judge a civilization good or bad according as it is or is not progressive. The ideals of liberty and democracy, which have their own ancient and independent justification, have sought a new strength by attaching themselves to Progress. The conjunctions of 'liberty and progress,' 'democracy and progress,' meet us at every turn. Socialism, at an early stage of its modern development, sought the same aid. The friends of Mars, who cannot bear the prospect of perpetual peace, maintain that war is an indispensable instrument of Progress. It is in the name of Progress that the doctrinaries who established the present reign of terror in Russia profess to act. All this shows the prevalent feeling that a social or political theory or programme is hardly tenable if it cannot claim that it harmonizes with this controlling idea."

In these changes called progress lies a hidden law not conceived by man and there are very few seers able to prophesy its future. I refer to the fact that every change conditions innumerable future changes. Again is progress social, mastery over nature, or mastery of human nature? Shaw declares the mastery over nature to be an illusion so far as progress is concerned.

"There is the illusion of 'increased command over Nature, meaning that the cotton is cheap and that ten miles of county road on a bicycle have replaced four on foot.' But even if man's increased command over Nature included any increased command over himself (the only sort of command relevant to his evolution into a higher being), the fact remains that it is only by running away from the increased command over Nature to country places where Nature is still in primitive command over Man that he can recover from the effects of the smoke, the ugliness, the dirt which the cheap cotton costs us."

Thus progress always is becoming and never is. Action seems to exist only to beget other action. Do we live now or in some future? The meaning of heaven has been supplanted by the aim of living for the next generation. But what does the next generation live for when it arrives? The same thing *ad infinitum*. Even in our modern civilization, with many people, selling tickets to heaven is progress. If you want to know whether we are making progress count the membership of the churches. Others measure progress by our charitable institutions. To look upon the bread and butter side of life as the measure of progress gets us nowhere so far as a mastery of our savage animal nature is concerned. Yet this concrete objective selfish appeal will be the measure of progress to the majority who have lost sight of and faith in the gold paved streets. It seems impossible to get any common agreement even on the direction of progress. The title of a recent book is *Where Are We Going*.

Kilpatrick sums it up well in a paragraph, in his *Source Book in Philosophy of Education*.

"In still clearer fashion is the term *progress* relative to man. In time of war the 'advancing' battle front is evidently progress. Not so with the 'retreating' line; one cannot call that progress which to him means destruction and defeat. The same battle line is then differently named according as it is differently viewed. Progress is thus a term applied by anyone to a process when he approves the result. For unwelcome results, such terms as retrogression, degeneration, and the like, are deemed appropriate. Progress then being an approved process has all the relativity that belongs to process and more besides; for no man uses the term progress unless he himself approves the end toward which the process is judged to be tending."

WHAT IS THE GOOD LIFE? Literature should uphold the good life, so says the educational world. In commending and condemning literature this *better life* is the subjective measure that each individual carries with him. On this subject whole volumes could be compiled, including an endless variety of ideas. But the mistake which most of these writers make is that of assuming that all others are like themselves or at least *could and should be made like them*. Gandhi would have us return to primitive conditions. He says: "Therein lies the salvation. People live long under such conditions, in comparative peace, much greater than Europe has enjoyed after having taken up modern activity."

Russell, in *Why Men Fight,* believes the inactive life intolerable. He says: "Desire, activity, purpose, are essential to a tolerable life, and a millennium, though it may be a joy in prospect, would be intolerable if it were actually achieved."

Socrates considered the good life to consist in "wanting as little as possible." The complement to this is Schopenhauer's idea that unhappiness results from the multiplication of desires, and that intensified consciousness multiplies unsatisfied desires. George Eliot, in her "Romola" says:

"We can only have the highest happiness, such as goes with being a great man, by having wide thoughts, and much feeling for the rest of the world as well as ourselves; and this sort of happiness often brings so much pain with it that we can only tell it from pain by its being what we would choose before everything else, because our souls see it is good."

Greek and Roman thought both centered about the

good life, but in different ways. Marcus Aurelius would
have us resign ourselves to the laws of Nature. It is the
subjective life.

"Be not disgusted, nor discouraged, nor dissatisfied,"
he says "if thou dost not succeed in doing everything
according to right principles; but when thou hast failed,
return back again, and be content if the greater part of
what thou doest is consistent with man's nature."

Epictetus also gives us a subjective view of the good
life.

"Men are disturbed not by things, but by the views
which they take of things. Thus death is nothing terrible,
else it would have appeared so to Socrates. But the terror
consists in our notion of death, that it is terrible. When,
therefore, we are hindered, or disturbed, or grieved let
us never impute it to others, but to ourselves; that is,
to our own views. It is the action of an uninstructed
person to reproach others for his own misfortunes; of
one entering upon instruction, to reproach himself; and
of one perfectly instructed, to reproach neither others nor
himself.

"Demand not that events should happen as you wish;
but wish them to happen as they do happen, and you will
go on well." [47]

Plato's Dialogues must be classed both as literature and
as philosophy. His famous notion of happiness as the
contemplation of the beautiful is best set forth in the
Symposium. Among the many points of view here is one
piece of advice as to how to grow into this state of spiritual contemplation.

"He who would proceed aright in this matter should
begin in youth to visit beautiful forms; and first, if he
be guided by his instructor aright, to love one such form
only—out of that he should create fair thoughts; and

soon he will of himself perceive that the beauty of one form is akin to the beauty of another; and then if beauty of form in general is his pursuit, how foolish would he be not to recognize that the beauty in every form is one and the same! And when he perceives this he will abate his violent love of the one, which he will despise and deem a small thing, and will become a lover of all beautiful forms; in the next stage he will consider that the beauty of the mind is more honorable than the beauty of the outward form. So that if a virtuous soul have but a little comeliness, he will be content to love and tend him, and will search out and bring to birth the thoughts which may improve the young, until he is compelled to contemplate and see the beauty of institutions and laws, and to understand that the beauty of them all is of one family, and that personal beauty is a trifle; and after laws and institutions he will go on to the sciences, that he may see their beauty, being not like a servant in love with the beauty of one youth or man or institution, himself a slave mean and narrow-minded, but drawing toward and contemplating the vast sea of beauty, he will create many fair and noble thoughts and notions in boundless love of wisdom; until that shore he grows and waxes strong, and at last the vision is revealed to him of a single science, which is the science of beauty everywhere.)" [48]

I repeat that the primary trouble with all these advocates is the fact that each makes his own subjective state the standard for all others. Only Marcus Aurelius saw clearly that each one must act according to his own nature.

THE BIGNESS OF GREAT LITERARY MINDS. We have already seen the growing appreciation of early Hindu thinking. But the average writer and reader has yet a long way to travel. I have already referred to and quoted from Dutt's excellent translation of the two great Epics of India. Max Müller, scholar and thinker, first opened the eyes of the modern world to the various systems of philosophy buried in Hindu literature.

Ramayana [49] gave religion and theology something to think about. It is a great poem of devotion to truth and duty in which scarcely a single person falters or complains. Its treatment of human problems and its portrayal of character will live forever.

Behind it lies no narrow-minded philosophy, but an open-mindedness that tolerates all kinds of beliefs. The poet relates a speech of a skeptic that sounds like Omar Khayyam or some of our modern dramatists.

I have already said that Plato's Dialogues are excellent as literature. But they are also psychology which culminates in philosophy. That philosophy is the well-known doctrine of ideas. Ideas constitute the only real existence. Our senses delude and deceive us. In the chapter on symbolism we have already outlined his philosophical allegory of the Cave—the greatest ever written. It is found in the ninth book of *The Republic*. It denies the reality of the objective world. The last ten years of science has almost done the same thing. Here are also found the modern ideas of socialism and of equality of the sexes. Emerson once said that out of Plato came all things that are now written and debated among men.

Euripides was a modern socialistic philosopher. He would place all morals on a basis of reason and intelligence. He blots out the gap between the finite and the infinite. But that which lies beyond human knowledge is a field for speculation and wonder. About thirty years ago Coleridge presented to the public, in a two volume edition, twenty plays of Euripides. Through them all runs the thread of Fate, Destiny. This fate is not a Presbyterian foundation: it is the fate of natural law within which man's deeds operate—the unforseen and unbroken chain of events. In *Hippolytus* we find the Nurse of Phaedra saying:

"Better be sick than tend the sick; the first is but a single ill, the last unites mental grief with manual toil. Man's whole life is full of anguish; no respite from his woes he finds; but if there is aught to love beyond this life, night's dark pall doth wrap it round. And so we show our mad love of this life because its light is shed on earth, and because we know no other, and have naught revealed to us of all our earth may hide; and trusting to fables we drift at random."

In that striking play called *Helen,* superstition and the prostitution of human intelligence receive one severe blow after another. But nowhere in this rebellion is it so evident as in the culmination of the conversation between Menelaus and the messenger.

"MES. It shall be done, O king. Now I see how worthless are the seer's tricks, how full of falsehood; nor is there after all aught trustworthy in the blaze of sacrifice or in the cry of feathered fowls; 'tis folly, the very notion that birds can help mankind. Calchas never by word or sign showed the host the truth, when he saw his friends dying on behalf of a phantom, nor yet did Helenus; but the city was stormed in vain. Perhaps thou wilt say 'twas not heaven's will that they should do so. Then why do we employ these prophets? Better were it to sacrifice to the gods, and crave a blessing, leaving prophecy alone; for this was but devised as a bait to catch a livelihood, and no man grows rich by divination if he is idle. No! sound judgment and disconcernment are the best of seers."

In that powerful tragedy *Heracles Mad,* the Chorus of Old Men try to induce Heracles to give up the struggle.

They tell him how the gods violate law and order and brave the issue of their crimes. They promise him lands and gifts, all in vain. Heracles replies:

"Tush! this is quite beside the question of my troubles. For my part, I do not believe that the gods indulge in unholy unions; and as for putting fetters on parents' hands, I have never thought that worthy of credit, nor will I now be so persuaded, not again that one god is naturally lord and master of another. For the deity, if he be really such, has no wants; these are miserable fictions of the poets. But I, for all my piteous plight reflected whether I should let myself be branded as a coward for giving up my life. For whoso schooleth not his frail mortal nature to bear fate's buffets as he ought, will never be able to withstand even a man's weapon. I will harden my heart against death and seek thy city, with grateful thanks for all thou offerest me."

Sophocles, born 497 B.C., shook himself loose from the superstitions of his time. He is a completely disillusioned man. Fate without moral order reigns supreme. He sees nature and life in its totality as one process. He makes one of his characters say: "Human life, even in its utmost splendor, hangs on the edge of a precipice." All this he saw without being a cynic. He believed that man, through his intelligence, could create some form of justice, moral order and beauty as well as triumph over nature. While man is a part of nature yet man's intelligence sets him above blind nature. Man's reason is to give order to the chaos of the universe.

He saw this mastery of nature and discovery of truth as a gradual unfolding process. In his *Antigone* Haemon, the son of Creon, King of Thebes, says:

"Father, the gods implant reason in men, the highest of all things that we call our own, Not mine the skill— far from me be the quest!—to say wherein thou speakest not aright; and yet another man, too, might have some useful thought. At least, it is my natural office to watch, on thy behalf, all that men say, or do, or find to blame. For the dread of thy frown forbids the citizen to speak such words as would offend thine ear; but I can hear these murmurs in the dark, these moanings of the city for this maiden."

Still more powerful is the language of the messenger in the same play!

"Dwellers by the house of Cadmus and of Amphion, there is no estate of mortal life that I would ever praise or blame as settled. Fortune raises and Fortune humbles the lucky or unlucky from day to day, and no one can prophesy to men concerning those things which are established. For Creon was best once, as I count bliss; he had saved this land of Cadmus from its foes; he was clothed with sole dominion in the land; he reigned, the glorious sire of princely children. And now all hath been lost. For when a man hath forfeited his pleasures, I count him not as living,—I hold him but a breathing corpse. Heap up riches in thy house, if thou wilt; live in kingly state; yet, if there be no gladness therewith, I would not give the shadow of a vapor for all the rest, compared with joy." [50]

Aeschylus leaned to problems of conduct, to questions of guilt and justice—even divine justice. He accepted some order of the universe—some teleological purpose. Yet the same old problem of Fate hung over him. In *Prometheus Bound* we read:

"*PROM*. It is not thus that Fate's decree is fixed; But I, long crushed with twice ten thousand woes
And bitter pains, shall then escape my bonds:
Art is far weaker than Necessity.

CHOR. Who guides the helm, then, of Necessity?
PROM. Fates triple-formed, Errinyes unforgetting.
CHOR. Is Zeus, then weaker in his might than these?
PROM. Not even He can 'scape the thing decreed.
CHOR. What is decreed for Zeus but still to reign?
PROM. Thou may'st no further learn, ask thou no more.
CHOR. 'Tis doubtless some dread secret which thou hidest.
PROM. Of other theme make mention, for the time
Is not yet come to utter this, but still
It must be hidden to the uttermost;
For by thus keeping it, it is that I
Escape my bandage foul, and these my pains." [51]

Dante's *Divine Comedy* is a mild compromise with the scholasticism of the Middle Ages. No student of Dante will mistake his striking symbolism. His philosophy is a modified rationalism.

Virgil represents sense-knowledge and human reason. It is shown to be adequate for guiding us through the hell of the entangled emotions. But concerning the supernatural, divine inspiration is needed. Beatrice is symbolic of this form of knowledge.

The other philosophical doctrine which absorbed Dante is the freedom of the will. This is the foundation of most religions, especially Catholicism. But modern biology, psychology, and sociology have completely undermined this supposed foundation of personal responsibility and salvation through personal will.

Goethe's extensive writings contain many philosophical suggestions and leave little doubt as to the philosophy lying back of his thinking. Indeed he tells us that when only a boy the Lisbon Earthquake turned loose questions which were not completely answered in a lifetime.

We have already commented on the fact that Goethe was influenced by the Pantheism of his time. Spinoza had already attracted the attention of the whole thinking world. He set forth the doctrine that God is all and in all. He looked on evil only as good out of which we have evolved.

"Faust.

Thy name?

Mephistopheles.

The question trifling seems from one,
Who it appears the Word doth rate so low;
Who, undeluded by mere outward show,
To Being's depth would penetrate alone.

Faust.

With gentlemen like you indeed
The inward essence from the name we read,
As all too plainly it doth appear,
When Beelzebub, Destroyer, Liar, meets the ear.
Who then art thou?

Mephistopheles.

Part of that power which still
Produceth good, whilst ever scheming ill.

Faust.

What hidden mystery in this riddle lies?

Mephistopheles.

I am the spirit who evermore denies!
And justly; for whate'er to light is brought
Deserves again to be reduced to naught;
Then better 'twere that naught should be.

Thus all the elements which ye
Destruction, Sin, or briefly, Evil, name,
As my peculiar element I claim.

Faust.

Thou nam'st thyself a part, and yet a whole I see.

Mephistopheles.

The modest truth I speak to thee.
Though folly's microcosm, man, it seems,
Himself to be a perfect whole esteems,
Part of the part am I, which at the first was all."

Ibsen was an individualist who, like Socrates, was far more interested in practical honesty and moral reform than in any philosophical theories of the universe. But as we have already seen he accepted modern evolution and made use of the idea. In *Brand* Ibsen comes as near suggesting some philosophical background as in any play. But even this is mostly a denial of the current religious ideas. In the first act Brand tells Einar that he is getting ready for a funeral. Einar says: "Who is it you bury?" Brand replies: "The God of whom you are so proud."

But the earth-bound, Socratic Ibsen whose chief interest is in showing us life—life as it is here and now—reaches a climax in *The Wild Duck*—a gloomy and powerful play with no outstanding ethical character, the weak hero struggling against a hopeless combination of heredity, tradition, social conditions, and self-distrust and condemnation. In *The Wild Duck* Ibsen decorates every page with unanswered questions. It is in most striking contrast to *The Enemy of the People*, to *Brand*, to *The Doll's House*. Its symbolism is subtle, especially that of the lame wild duck. Indeed it may symbolize almost every crippled character in the play—are all ethically wounded and caught in the power of environment. The realization of one's mission in life and in what he will find his highest happiness is now by no means psychologically or philosophically clear. *The Wild Duck* is a bitter irony on the emotional hot-headed reformer who madly reforms without any sense of the inevitable reaction.

No one can mistake the kinship between Nietzsche and Strindberg. Yet each was himself, not another—a bold independent thinker—dissecting human life. Each is in a measure a mystery among geniuses. When he makes one of his characters say: "It is the age you have warred against—it is the lord of the age, it is God who has crushed you," Strindberg sounds like Nietzsche crying out:

"Beware of the good and just! They would fain crucify those who invent their own standard of virtue—they hate the lonely one."

CHAPTER XIX

PHILOSOPHY IN LITERATURE (CONTINUED)

AUGUST STRINDBERG. Philosophically Strindberg should be classified as a strict naturalist. His powerful tragedy, *The Father,* is naturalism intensified. It is not adulterated by any of Maeterlinck's pervading spirit of the supernatural, although in form and structure he was much influenced by Maeterlinck. After all, instinct and biological urges guide the world—not human speculation. Strindberg saw how these underlying forces guide our reasoning about our conduct.

Starting as an extreme individualist Strindberg ends as the supreme universalist. Like Descartes he believed that the road to spiritual development and progress is in doubting and questioning. But, unlike Descartes, he never arrived at that certainty that made Descartes outstanding for a century. He remained a skeptic, accepting the doctrine of the relativity of all truth. He saw life as the result of a great network of interacting forces, and realized that the individual is a part of the vast universe and that he has no inalienable right to happiness.

ROBERT BROWNING. Browning, like Wordsworth, was nature's philosophical poet. Both were pantheistic. The chief difference is found in the fact that Wordsworth maintains a closer relation between nature, the universe and man than did Browning. Coleridge and Tennyson both approximate the same view. Nature for

Browning is a form of God's creation. Wordsworth seems to have been influenced by Leibnitz's "pre-established harmony" between body and mind. For Wordsworth this pre-established harmony between humanity and nature enables us to converse with nature. While Coleridge in speaking of nature says: "Her life the eddying of our living soul"—this sounds like Fichte's subjective idealism. The father of American psychology—G. Stanley Hall—must have had in mind ideas similar to those of Browning and Wordsworth when he briefly characterized his philosophy as "a higher monism where mind is subjective nature and nature is objectified mind."

> "He climbed to the top of Calvano,
>   And God's own profound
> Was above me, and round me the mountains,
>   And under, the sea,
> And within me my heart to bear witness
>   What was and shall be."

All his life, Browning held definite ideas about human nature, the purpose of human life, and man's relation to God. These he set forth definitely in the long poem, *Paracelsus*. He once said that he sought to understand: "God and his works and all God's intercourse with the human soul." He believed that we should develop as much as possible in this life as a preparation for another. This is the Socratic and Platonic view. Our failures keep alive our discontent. We must work within our limitations. The God within us is discontent. But we must frankly admit that the time has passed for Browning's philosophy to furnish any great challenge to the thinking world.

PERCY BYSSHE SHELLEY. Let us now turn our attention to Shelly, whose philosophy is simple, sweeping, and compelling. He entertains and fascinates as his sweeping philosophy unfolds behind his symbolism. His greatest work, at least from this standpoint, is *Prometheus Unbound*. Prometheus represents humanity, especially the human mind and will. The Earth is his mother. His kind and loving nature he gets from his mother extends even to the point of showing sympathy for his chief enemy—Jove. Jove is the anthropomorphic God of religion—the God of heaven. But the mind of man created him and delegated him all the power he has.

In turn Jove put Prometheus—Humanity—in chains, tormented him and oppressed mankind. The mind and will of man is enslaved so long as this god rules by delegated power.

In the first powerful act Prometheus is left chained to a cliff of rocks. Prometheus seeks to recall the curse he pronounced on Jove and which all nature applauded, but Prometheus will not divulge the secret which would save Jove from ruin.

His mother, the Earth, sends the spirits of heroes, of faith, and hope to cheer him. His wife is Asia—the symbol of love in Nature. The love element in nature must be united to the love element in man. The love spirit in nature protests against this enslavement of man by man's own creation. Finally the many forces struggling to free Prometheus are joined by Demogorgon—Eternity—and Jove is consigned to unending nothingness.

Prometheus Unbound is not simply a string of pleasing imagery. It is a powerful philosophical and ethical view of the world and of humanity. The author sees the evil in human nature, but the cure exists in man himself—it is the ideal of love and endurance. The universe is one with the moral strivings of man.[52]

The play opens with the speech of Prometheus, setting forth to some length his awful plight. In part he says:

"No change, no pause, no hope! Yet I endure.
I ask the Earth, have not the mountains felt?
I ask you Heaven, the all-beholding Sun,
Has it not seen? The Sea, in storm or calm,
Heaven's ever-changing Shadow, spread below,
Have its deaf waves not heard my agony?
Ah me! alas, pain, pain ever, for ever!"

Among the many messengers to Prometheus is a Fury
who describes the dilemma of the human heart as follows:

"In each human heart terror survives
The ruin it has gorged; the loftiest fear
All that they would disdain to think were true;
Hypocrisy and custom make their minds
The fanes of many a worship, now outworn.
They dare not devise good for man's estate,
And yet they know not that they do not dare."

Finally Demogorgon descends and moves toward the
throne of Jupiter. Then follows the final condemnation
and Jupiter's response.

Demogorgon.
    Eternity. Demand no direr name.
    Descend, and follow me down the abyss.
    I am thy child, as thou were Saturn's child;
    Mightier than thee; and we must dwell together
    Henceforth in darkness. Lift thy lightnings not.
    The tyranny of heaven none may retain,
    Or reassume, or hold, succeeding thee;
    Yet if thou wilt, as 'tis the destiny
    Of trodden worms to writhe till they are dead,
    Put forth thy might.

Prometheus is freed. All Nature rejoices and the proper union between man and Nature ultimately results. We might digress and discuss the similarity and relation of this philosophy to those of Wordsworth, Coleridge, Keats, and Browning. Or we might take a look at Spinoza shining through the whole of it. At least we might admit that it is pleasingly put and contains much true psychology.

GEORGE BERNARD SHAW. In studying a discussion of a subject as wide as philosophy in literature the reader will naturally ask why we select this or that piece of literature? There are several reasons for such selections. In the first place, the chief aim of the whole work has been to open up new ways of treating literature, to create interest, and to make easier the reading of certain types of literature. Again, certain problems and their solution are in the background guiding the selection. We select Shaw because he is without doubt the most outstanding English dramatist of this generation. Also there seems to be some definite philosophy behind his writings.

Few men live to see such a searching biography of themselves as Bernard Shaw now has. That book is Archibald Henderson's *George Bernard Shaw: His Life and Works*. I wish to acknowledge my indebtedness to this scholar and brilliant writer. I confess that for many years of my reading I did not take Shaw seriously—not until the appearance of *Man and Superman,* in 1903.

I had not grasped his skillful psychological play with the public. His work on art and music set me to a study of the man. I soon learned that he is not the arrogant egotist that some of my intellectual friends thought him to be. I saw that this is only a psychological smoke-screen used to mystify the public. He once said: "The art of humbug is the art of getting invented in this way." He believed that the public loves to be humbugged. I should rather say that the public loves to be kept excited, guessing.

Anyway in some cases it pays to study the life of a writer before studying his works.

Before Shaw was fifteen he knew well the chief musical geniuses of the world. He was a skilful player, which helped to give him a start in many ways. He studied art from many angles. He studied and used the modern sciences of evolution, physics, and chemistry. He served his day as a laborer to relieve the poverty of his parents. He undertook to become a public speaker and made as bad a failure of it as Demosthenes did. But he never stopped until he had mastered the art. His great versatility has made him a world author.

In his efforts to reach the public he was much like Ibsen. When Ibsen's great work *Brand* fell a prey to the word-critics who said that he knew nothing about poetry, he replied: "Do not think that I am an arrogant fool. In my private moments I probe my inner most parts. My book is poetry. If it is not it will be. The conception of poetry in Norway shall be made to conform to the book. In the world of ideal there is no stability."

Nothing could better express Bernard Shaw's attitude to the public. He said as much in his remarks on "the spontaneous recognition of really original work." Later he said: "I find that the surest way is to startle the world with daring innovations and originalities."

Now let us examine some of the theories and philosophies that underlie this versatile writer. In the first place he was himself disillusioned about human life and religion and has always tried to disillusion humanity. Thus while he seems to play with the public he is serious to the limit. In early life he became antagonistic to religion and boldly said when only sixteen that if what Moody and Sankey preached was religion he preferred atheism. He sees religion as preaching a doctrine of brotherhood and and practicing antagonism.

Shaw is a peaceful intellectual socialist. He is opposed to emotional unthinking revolutionary socialism. He anticipates that social improvement must grow out of economic conditions guided by human intelligence. Shaw does not look to the universities for progressive thinking. Even where they have departed from the old beliefs they lead men to believe rather than to think.

He is a psychologist, looking for the deeper forces lying behind convention and custom. In short he is a strict evolutionist. Some have said that his philosophy is an echo or elaboration of Nietzsche, Schopenhauer, and Ibsen. But he is more than an echo. Shaw is too much of a genius to be dominated by anyone's opinions. True he has always been a strong advocate of Ibsen, and a bitter critic of Shakespeare for having no philosophical conception of life.

Shaw's *Man and Superman* would seem to look back to Schopenhauer and Nietzsche. But the views of these men are modified or supplemented by the ideas in Bergsen's *Creative Evolution*. Shaw, like Tolstoy, was interested in creating a new religion—a religion for evolution. This he presents in the third act of *Man and Superman*. Here he identifies God with the life force. This life force is not perfect, but is struggling to become perfect. He answers the question asked by millions: "Why, if God is all-powerful and merciful, does He tolerate such calamities as wars, disasters of all kinds, and the suffering of mankind?" He replies that God is not all wise, all powerful. During the whole of time He has been experimenting to find the best instrument to perfection. Man is his last experiment. If man fails he will be scrapped also. He says: "You should live so that when you die God is in your debt."

When Benjamin Franklin was only a youth he interrogated the New England clergy as to the chief attributes of God. He received the common theological answer: all-wise, all-powerful, and all-good. He then produced a pamphlet in which he demonstrated that, if these are true, then the world is perfect and we have no right to interfere with it.

In *Candida* Shaw shows his preference for "natural instinct" as a guide to conduct. This life force is the essence of the universe, but it is not a blind will like that of Schopenhauer—it is a purposeful will.

Ibsen is not alone in his struggles to solve the psychological problem of the freedom of the will. It has been one of the chief philosophical problems for Shaw. After setting three definite necessary limits to it he found nothing of freedom left even in himself. He feels that there is something deeper than conscious will back of life and conduct. He expressed this definite idea often, but never plainer than when he read a paper on Darwin and Lamarck.

"My life has been a miraculous transformation of a good-for-nothing boy into the writer of this paper, and of several quite unaccountable, uncommercial plays through a mysterious will in me, which has prevailed over environment, heredity and every sort of external discouragement. What is more, that will is not me: it makes the merest instrument of me—often overworks and abuses me most unreasonably. It makes me perform the feats of a bold, energetic, resourceful man, though I am actually a timid, lazy, unready one. It makes me write things before I understand them; and I am conscious that my own subsequent attempts to explain them are sometimes lame and doubtful."

EUGENE O'NEILL. In conclusion we must give a brief consideration to our greatest American dramatist—

Eugene O'Neill—that unique original thinker who apparently sees life both as comedy and tragedy. "We are tragic figures, and also fit subjects for the highest comedy, were one sufficiently detached to write it." This strange philosophy of life and his original way of putting it has attracted the attention of world thinkers. In spite of criticisms of pessimism he pushes on with an unquenched fire. Twice he won the Pulitzer Prize for the best American work of the year—*Beyond the Horizon,* in 1920 and *Anna Christie* in 1921.

He is a psychologist of a high order—a Strindberg, but with a philosophy lying behind his psychology which is not easy to fathom. It is a modification of the old naturalism that leans toward the supernatural or a higher naturalism. He is reaching out for something beyond or behind life. He is struggling against realism, yet avoiding the loose supernatural that led Maeterlinck astray.

The accusation of being pessimistic is best expressed in his own words and at the same time this paragraph gives an insight into his view of life.

"I have been accused of unmitigated gloom. Is this pessimistic? I do not think so. . . . To me, the tragic alone has that significant beauty which is truth. It is the meaning of life—and the hope. The noblest is eternally the most tragic. The people who succeed and do not push on to a greater failure are the spiritual middle classes. Their stopping at success is the proof of their compromising insignificance. How pretty their dreams must have been! The man who pursues the mere attainable should be sentenced to get it—and keep it. Let him rest on his laurels and enthrone him in a Morris chair, in which laurels and hero may wither away together. Only through the unattainable does man achieve a hope worth living

and dying for—and so attain himself. He with the
spiritual guerdon of a hope in hopelessness is near-
est to the stars and the rainbow's foot."

In the play *Lazarus Laughed* he characterized Lazarus
as being dominated by the will to live, not for himself
but for man in general. In spite of the charge of pessimism his philosophy is optimistic. His sharp distinction
between man and men expresses itself thus:

"Believe! What if you are a man and men are despic-
able? Men are also unimportant! Men pass! Like rain
into the sea! The sea remains! Man remains! Man slowly
arises from the part of the race of men that was his tomb
of death! For Man death is not! Son of God's laughter,
is!"

It was a master stroke when *Strange Interlude* had
four characters come on the stage and reveal their inner
thoughts as if they were alone and thinking out loud,
giving an insight into their deeper life through a period
of some twenty-seven years. All the critical points of
their private inner lives are laid bare. O'Neill shows an
amazing ability to understand the complexities of the
human heart. He is searching for the fountains of human
activity and conduct.

The Great God Brown is a bitter attack on materialism
as represented in Brown. It represents man at war with
himself. Man does not know himself. Only Cybel who is
symbolic of mother earth knows him.

OTHER CONSIDERATIONS. We might elaborate
upon the supernatural background we have already seen
in Maeterlinck. We might pry into the socialistic philosophy of Galsworthy. We might attempt to unearth the
philosophy of that strange and original poet and dramatist
—Stephen Phillips. He is worthy of any one's interest
and study. Nearly all his writings are founded on Greek

material, but given a modern meaning in a modern setting. His *Ulysses* indicates that virtue has fled from the modern world. His *Armageddon,* published in 1915 was a burning satire on the World War. The scene is laid in Hell. The inhabitants are tired of the monotony and ask the Devil what they can do to create some excitement. He suggests war. But he tells them that there is only one way to start a war and to keep it going—everybody must lie about everybody else and if any one refuses he must be shot.

We might even ask if any philosophy of life and the universe underlies the works of Shakespeare. So many volumes have been written on this subject directly or indirectly that I refuse to enter this vast field. As a psychologist he stands supreme. But philosophy of life and the universe is another thing. We have already seen how he, in common with all great writers, wrestled with the problem of personal freedom. He found it limited within by heredity and without by habit, convention, and general conditions. Many phases of his work seem to indicate some faith in some kind of a supernatural. But here it is hard to distinguish between the current beliefs and superstitions skillfully used and any real acceptance of such views. *The Tempest* and *Midsummer-Night's Dream* are saturated with ideas of this kind. But these plays intentionally go beyond real life. Outside of these and other constant indications of some outside force or knowing spirits I fail to discover anything that may be called a philosophy in the sense that it answers the three questions of What? How? and Why?

Now if I have succeeded in convincing the reader that to have some idea of the underlying philosophy of life is at least a help in reading certain types of literature and that it may render such reading more pleasurable and thought provoking, the object of these two chapters has been accomplished. As I have said about psychology in literature, the glory of great writers is that they leave us so many different possible interpretations. For this reason I disown any dogmatic interpretation in this book.

To me the most important discovery of modern science is the *universality, constancy,* and *sameness* of certain fundamental elements in human nature that have made all the general behavior, wars, governments, institutions, morals, and religions. Of this I think I find ample proof in the great literatures of the world.

NOTES

1. See *Descent of Man*, Volume 2.
2. Dewey and McClellan—*Psychology of Number*, Macmillan Co.
3. *American Journal of Psychology*, 1896.
4. Kilpatrick, W. H.—*Creative School Music*, Burdett & Co.
5. Stevenson, B. E.—*Home Book of Verse for Young Folks*, Henry Holt & Co.
6. Lincoln Kirstein—*Dance*, 1935, Putnam's Sons.
7. Hazel Gertrude Kinscella—*Music on the Air*, Silver Burdett & Co.
8. A. H. Verrill—*The American Indian*.
9. Winifred Turner—*Great Schools of Painting*.
10. Bryant—*Odyssey of Homer*, Mifflin Co.
11-12. *Gospel Stories*, Crowell & Co.
13. Olive Schreiner—*Dreams*. M. A. Donohue and Co.
14. Friedrich Nietzsche—*Thus Spake Zarathustra*, Macmillan Co.
15. Caroline Augusta Davids—*Buddhist Psychology*, edited by D. R. S. Mead, Macmillan Co.
16. Paul Carus—*Gospel of Buddha*, Open Court Co.
17. George H. Lewes—*Biographical History of Philosophy*, Appleton & Co.
18. Henrich Ibsen—*Plays*, tr. Archer, Scribner's Sons.
19. Longfellow—*Dante's Divine Comedy*, Mifflin & Co.
20. Ibsen—*Little Eyolf*, p. 76.
21. Goethe—*Faust*, Dana, Estes and Co.
22. Plato—*Republic*, tr. Jowett.
23. Anton Chekhov—*The Cherry Orchard*, tr. George Calderson, Mitchell Kennerley Co.
24. Shakespeare—*Hamlet*, p. 73, F. M. Dent & Co.
25. Romesh C. Dutt—*Great Epics of Ancient India*, p. 250, Dent & Sons.
26. Gerhart Hauptmann—*The Weavers*, tr. R. H. Russell, Harper & Brothers.
27. William James—*Varieties of Religious Experiences*.
28. Goethe—*Sorrows of Werther*, p. 9, 12, and 13, Dana, Estes & Co.
29. Euripides—*The Plays Vol. I and II*, George Bell and Sons.
30. D. E. Phillips—*Elementary Psychology*, p. 300, Ginn & Co.

31. Friedrich Nietzsche—*Thus Spake Zarathustra*, p. 222, tr. A. Tille, Macmillan Co.

32. August Strindberg—*Plays*, p. 114, tr. R. M. Savage, Boni and Liveright.

33. *The Open Court*, p. 431.

34. Mark Twain—*The Mysterious Stranger*, p. 95-99, Harper & Bros.

35. James Cabell—*Beyond Life*, p. 50-52, Boni and Liveright.

36. Anton Chekhov—*The Sea Gull, Two Plays*, 53, Mitchell Kennerley Co.

37. Robert Browning—*Ring and the Book*, p. 240-242, Crowell & Co.

38. *The Open Court*, Nov. 1929, p. 646-656.

39. Victor Hugo—*Les Miserables*, Henry Coates & Co.

40. Winston Churchill—*The Inside of the Cup*, p. 5-7, Macmillan Co.

41. *Ramayana*, tr. Dutt, p. 151.

42. Henrich Ibsen—*Ghosts*, tr. Archer, Scribner's Sons.

43. August Strindberg—*Countess Julie*, Mother Earth Publishing Association.

44. Emma Goldman—*The Modern Drama*, p. 125 and 126, Richard G. Badger.

45. Emma Goldman—*The Modern Drama*, p. 202 and 203.

46. W. B. Yeats—*Where There is Nothing*, Macmillan Co.

47. Bakewell—*Ancient Philosophy*, Scribner's Sons.

48. Plato—*Symposium*, tr. by Jowett, p. 210-212.

49. Dutt—*Ramayana*, p. 60 and 61.

50. *Plays of Euripides*, Vol. I, p. 345 and Vol. II, p. 213, George Bell and Sons.

51. *Plays of Aeschylus*, tr. Plumptre, p. 136 and 137, Heath & Co.

52. Shelley—*Poems*, Vol. I, p. 396-445, P. F. Collier & Sons.

ACKNOWLEDGMENTS

The author is grateful to the following publishers and authors for permission to quote from their works as follows:

To Simon & Schuster, Inc., for *Treasury of the Theatre;* to Silver Burdett Co., for *Creative Music,* by Fox and Hopkins; to James Branch Cabell, for *Beyond Life;* to John W. Luce and Co., for *The Father,* by Strindberg, tr. by Oland; to Charles Scribner's Sons, for *Ibsen's Plays,* tr. by Archer, for *The Blue Flower* by Van Dyke, and for *Plays* by Strindberg, tr. by Bjorkman; to L. C. Page & Co., for *Faust* and *Sorrows of Werther,* by Goethe, tr. by Anna Swanwick; to the Open Court Publishing Co., for *Gospel of Buddha,* by Carus; to D. C. Heath & Co., for works of Sophocles and Aeschylus, tr. by Plumptre; to G. P. Putnam's Sons, for *The Dance,* by Kirstein, and for *The Diamond Necklace,* by Guy de Maupassant; to D. Appleton-Century Co., for *Biographical History of Philosophy,* by Lewis, and for *My Childhood,* by Gorky; to Oliver Huckel, for *The Dusk of the Gods,* by Wagner; to Columbia University Press, for *Modern Fiction,* by Brewster and Burrell; to Thomas Y. Crowell Co., for Tolstoy's *Gospel Stories;* to the Macmillan Co., for *Thus Spoke Zarathustra,* by Nietzsche, tr. by Tille, for *The Inside of the Cup,* by Churchill, and for *The Source Book in Philosophy of Education,* by Kilpatrick; to Harper & Bros., for *The Mysterious Stranger,* by Mark Twain; to Longmans, Green & Co., for *Six Systems of Hindu Philosophy,* by Max Müller; to Houghton

Mifflin, for *The Divine Comedy,* by Dante, tr. by Longfellow; to Chapman & Grimes, for *The Modern Drama,* by Goldman; to J. M. Dent & Sons, for *Ramayana* and *Mahabharata;* to the Viking Press, for *The Weavers* from *The Dramatic Works of Hauptmann,* tr. by Russell; to Ginn & Co., for *An Elementary Psychology,* by D. E. Phillips; to C. Bell & Sons, Ltd., for *The Plays of Euripides,* tr. by Murray; to M. A. Donohue & Co., for *Dreams,* by Olive Schreiner; to Thomas Nelson & Sons, for *Rubaiyat of Omar Khayham,* tr. by Fitzgerald; to George Bernard Shaw, for *Three Plays for Puritans;* to Heinemann Company, for Lawrence Hope's *Last Poems.*